BestMasters

Springer awards "BestMasters" to the best application-oriented master's theses, which were completed at renowned chairs of economic sciences in Germany, Austria and Switzerland in 2013.
The works received highest marks and were recommended for publication by supervisors. As a rule, they show a high degree of application orientation and deal with current issues from different fields of economics.
The series addresses practitioners as well as scientists and offers guidance for early stage researchers.

Markus Vollmer

# A Beta-return Efficient Portfolio Optimisation Following the CAPM

## An Analysis of International Markets and Sectors

Springer Gabler

Markus Vollmer
Stuttgart, Germany

ISBN 978-3-658-06633-8 ISBN 978-3-658-06634-5 (eBook)
DOI 10.1007/978-3-658-06634-5

The Deutsche Nationalbibliothek lists this publication in the Deutsche Nationalbibliografie; detailed bibliographic data are available in the Internet at http://dnb.d-nb.de.

Library of Congress Control Number: 2014945108

Springer Gabler


Printed on acid-free paper

Springer Gabler is a brand of Springer DE.
Springer DE is part of Springer Science+Business Media.
www.springer-gabler.de

## Acknowledgements

Though only my name appears on the cover of this dissertation, a great many people have contributed to its production. I owe my gratitude to all those people who have made this dissertation possible and because of whom my graduate experience has been one that I will cherish forever.

My deepest gratitude is to my supervisor, Prof. Dr. Simon Gao. I have been amazingly fortunate to have an advisor who taught me how to verge on this voluminous research project. Furthermore, I appreciated his valuable support which I received within our meetings and his guidance even when I was back in Germany.

My co-supervisor, Prof. Dr. Tobias Popović, has been always there to listen and give content-related and personal advice. I am deeply grateful to him for the long discussions that helped me to sort out the structural details and also for his support by equipping me with recent academic literature.

Many friends have helped me stay sane through the demanding years of my graduate studies, foremost my long standing friends Benjamin Krotz, Malte Henn and Sebastian Honold (all graduates from HFT Stuttgart), my fellow students from Edinburgh Napier University, Hannes Gottschlich and Nico Zimmermann, and my best friend Miriam Gref. I greatly value their friendship and I deeply appreciate their belief in me. Most importantly, none of this would have been possible without the support and patience of my family. For this reason I dedicate this dissertation to my parents, my brother Frank and my beloved girlfriend Barbara who have been an instant source of love and strength all the times and in particular in the last six months.

# Table of Contents

## List of figures

# List of tables

## Abstract

### Purpose

The most widely used but also extensively debated method for pricing security return is the capital asset pricing model (CAPM). In combination with Markowitz's (1959) statement on the reduction of unsystematic risk through diversification, this dissertation focuses on the development of a risk-return efficient equity allocation.

### Design/methodology/approach

A quantitative research design is used which deductively employs the market index model and other grand theories as the foundation within the research process. A repeated cross-sectional analysis of the Global Stock Market is used to increase the validity and reliability of the findings to answer the research questions. The philosophies behind this approach are those of a functionalist, positivist and objectivist. The secondary data prohibits from biases connected with its sampling.

### Findings

First of all, the study found proof that noticeable differences exist between countries and supersectors in regards to the beta-return relationship. Secondly, the analysis of the data allows for a risk-return efficient equity allocation. Thirdly, the predictability of future single stock performance was weak and stock picking or market timing cannot be supported by the implemented beta-return ratio.

### Research Limitations

Even though the proxy is comprehensive it cannot be regarded as perfect because emerging economies are missing. Also, the statistical significance is limited due to the nature of the cross-sectional approach.

Finally, the validation of the findings is critical as the research about international and cross-sector stock market behaviour is scarce.

**Practical Implications**

The results of this work enable institutional and large private investors to optimise their stock portfolios through a beta-risk efficient diversification across sectors and countries.

**Originality/value**

This dissertation analyses one of the most comprehensive data sets available. Furthermore, it investigates more countries and industry sectors than all of the literature found on this topic.

# Chapter 1: Introduction

## 1.1 Chapter Introduction

This chapter delves into the background of this area of interest by giving a brief review. The reasons for conducting this research are explained and the goal of this work is stated, including the formulation of the research questions. Finally, the structure of this study is placed at the disposal.

## 1.2 Background and Problem Foundation

"There is no such thing as a free lunch" (Milton Friedman)

This quote was popularised by the same-titled book of the Sveriges Riksbank Prize in Economic Sciences in Memory of Alfred Nobel (henceforth: Nobel Prize) laureate Friedman (1975) who is best known for his contributions to price and monetary theory. This statement reflects the economic key concept of opportunity costs. Mankiw (2011) argues that when one likes to get one special thing, usually one must give up another. Regarding a portfolio the opportunity cost of higher returns is a higher risk exposure. Markowitz (1959), who was strongly influenced by his PhD-supervisor Friedman, states in his pioneering monograph about investment diversification:

> "A good portfolio is more than a long list of good stocks and bonds. It is a balanced whole, providing the investor with protections and opportunities with respect to a wide range of contingencies. The investor should build toward an integrated portfolio which best suits his needs." (Markowitz 1959, p.3).

The reasons a portfolio should be well-diversified have not become less important in recent years as the widely discussed study of Brinson *et al.* (1991) demonstrates. The researchers give evidence that the asset allocation is the most important factor for a long-term investment success and should be chosen over stock picking and market timing. This has been supported by the findings of Ibbotson & Kaplan (2000). While this kind of research focused on the whole investment portfolio including various asset classes, this dissertation concentrates on equity portfolios.

Based on the findings of Sharpe (1964), who created the Capital Asset Pricing Model (CAPM) for which he gained the Nobel Prize, the outcome of this study supports institutional and wealthy private investors to optimise their stock portfolios. Furthermore, the conducted research broadens the knowledge of academics and students on international stock markets.

The diversification across countries and sectors will be of special interest to reduce the unsystematic risk, because asset classes, countries and especially sectors show specific differences in their behaviour of risk and return.

The major hindrance to optimisation is the systematic risk of stocks. Sharpe (1964) recognised that a single factor can explain the cross-sectional differences of stock return – Beta, the covariance of the stock and the market return. This theory has been a hot subject to numerous studies which tested its empirical validity. If the theory holds true it should be possible to construct a risk-return efficient portfolio which integrates the reduction of systematic and unsystematic risk. While the unsystematic risk should be eliminated by diversification, the systematic risk should be reducible by the use of the beta-return ratio, a measure implemented within this work.

## 1.3 Aims and Objectives

The overall aim of the research is to construct a portfolio that earns a higher return and simultaneously comprises a lower systematic risk than the (global) market portfolio. Furthermore, the investigation uncovers imbalances between different economies and sectors in regard to investment advantageousness. This requires an examination of the global equity market to answer the following research questions:

RQ 1: Is it possible to determine differences among the international stock markets regarding the beta-return relationship?

RQ 2: Do industry-sector-specific differences exist with regard to the beta-return relationship?

RQ 3: What are the implications for an effective and efficient equity asset allocation?

RQ 4: Is it effective to build a future oriented investment strategy upon an ex-post data/return analysis?

## 1.4 Structure

Following the introductory part, the key findings and results of previous studies build on or driven from grand fundamental theories on the studied topic are presented and critically evaluated within the literature review. In chapter 3, the methodology used for this study is illustrated, including the approach, strategies, and methods. Chapter 4 presents the data analysis and the discussion on the findings. Finally, Chapter 5 provides the conclusions of the research conducted, its limitations and an outlook. Figure 1 illustrates the process and structure of this dissertation.

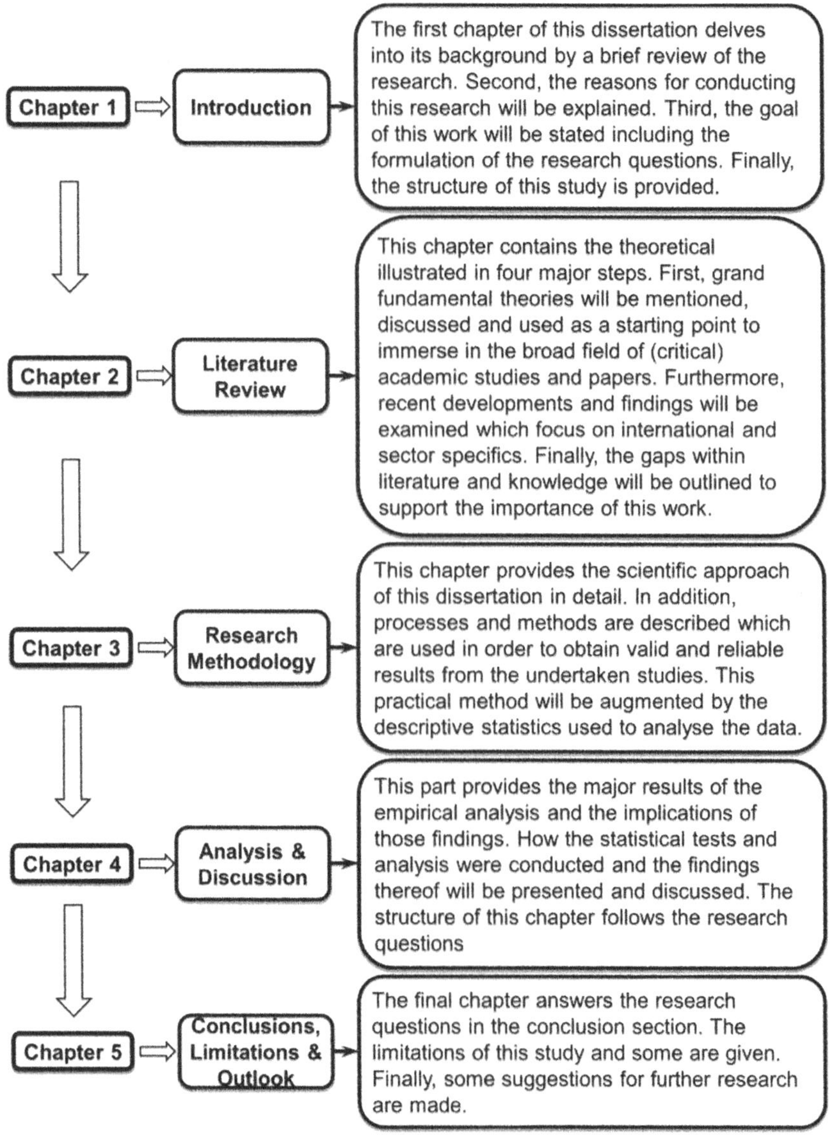


Figure 1: Disposition of the dissertation

# Chapter 2: Literature Review

## 2.1 Chapter Introduction

This chapter illustrates the theoretical framework of this dissertation in four major sections: Firstly grand fundamental theories on the cross-section of stock returns are discussed. Secondly deductive academic studies are critically reviewed. Thirdly, recent developments and findings are examined, focussing on international and sector specific aspects of the risk-return relationship. In the fourth section, gaps within the literature are outlined to support the importance of this dissertation.

## 2.2 Fundamental Theory

This work builds on different theories and important areas of study. As the existence of **efficient markets** is a basic assumption for asset-pricing models in general its analysis is conducted. Then, the importance of diversification and stock-picking is illustrated by having a close look at the **modern portfolio theory**. This is followed by a critical review of the **CAPM** which is deduced from the aforementioned theories in order to allocate the best securities within a portfolio. This will include the area of **Behavioural Finance** which tries to explain market anomalies. Furthermore, alternative **asset-pricing theories** which have been developed by the opponents of the CAPM are highlighted. Finally, international and sector specific research is presented in the section on **recent development**.

### *2.2.1 Efficient Markets*

Market efficiency is the basic assumption for asset pricing models. Cohen *et al.* (2009) proved that a joint hypothesis between the CAPM and market efficiency approximates the pricing of stocks well at price level for both growth and value securities. Therefore, this dissertation discusses the development and recent findings about the most important theories, the **Random walk hypothesis** and **efficient-market hypothesis**.

#### *2.2.1.1 Random Walk Hypothesis (RWH)*

The RWH finds its origin in the early works of Bachelier (1900).Extended and translated into English by Cootner (1964) this theory submits that stocks at the end of a certain time period largely show future prices. These seem to be generated by a random process and show independent (Gaussian or normal standard) distributions. Other chartist theories however share the common assumption that history repeats itself and therefore historical stock price behaviours can be used to predict a share's price (Fama 1965).

Bachelier (1900) and later Osborne (1959) inductively transferred botanic observations like the Brownian motion to build a mathematical model to explain price fluctuations on the stock market. Even though both tried to justify this theory empirically, they felt short as they only used cross-sectional data. Moore (1962), analysing only eight shares from the U.S. Stock market (NYSE), and Kendall (1953), examining 19 British industrial indices, deductively proved that successive stock prices cannot be predicted by adjusting historical prices. They observed an approximately normal distribution; however they acknowledged that most of the distributions were leptokurtic which weakens their findings. To provide more reliable facts, Fama (1965) analysed the whole Dow-Jones Industrial Average index (30 stocks). He was also able to explain the "fat tails" within his sample by using the findings of Mandelbrot (1963), who states that distributions show a stable Paretian (Levy 1925) shape with characteristic exponents smaller than 2.

The efficiency of information also plays a major role within this research area. If any information is distributed or accessible to/from each investor there would not be any fluctuation or variation in stock prices. Only when new information is created the market reacts (Fama 1965). If the market (buyers and sellers) knows about a company`s future, this would already be reflected in the current stock price (Samuelson 1965). As information is processed in different ways and there is existing disagreement about a company's intrinsic value stock prices fluctuate randomly. Fama (1965) calls it the market's "noise" and forms a fundament for short-term behavioural models like the one of Barberis *et al.* (1998). According to Fama (1998) this does not contradict the long-term market efficiency but underlines its power. One of the best established investment strategies, the long-term focussed *buy and hold* approach, is based on this idea. It is used to create an optimised portfolio according to the major aim of this dissertation.

Even though there is strong evidence provided by several renowned academics supporting the market efficiency of the RWH (Jensen 1978), Lo & MacKinlay (1988) rejected it with their quantitative analysis of 625 US stocks during a 1,216-week time period by applying a variance-ratio test. However, by increasing the observation interval from one to four weeks they were not able to reject the hypothesis. These findings raise the question if information is not incorporated fast enough or if there is too little information on small firms available to the market.

To summarise, a rapid incorporation of information leads to market efficiency where price changes are independent. These findings play a major role to create the different "levels" of market efficiency which are discussed in the following subsection.

#### *2.2.1.2 Efficient-Market Hypothesis (EMH)*

As Jensen (1978) states in his symposium the EMH has become an accepted fact within the financial literature. The major contribution of this hypothesis can be described as follows:

> "It is not possible to make economic profits in an efficient market by trading on the basis on an information set $\theta_t$ which is already given in the moment of trading."

The definition of the information set is the reason for different versions of the EMH: weak, semi-strong and strong. They were first mentioned by Roberts (1967) and have been tested and reviewed widely by various academics since (Jensen 1978, Dimson & Mussavian 1998, Fama 1998, Sewell 2011). The typology is defined as follows (Fama 1970, LeRoy 1989, Spremann 2008):

The information set in the **weak form** includes all historical stock prices at the time of the appraisal, public or private information is excluded. As this is given for all markets this form is not under consideration within the literature.

In the **semi-strong** set contains besides the historical prices all publicly available information (e.g. annual reports). Private information is excluded from this set.

A **strong form** of efficiency exists if the set comprises historical prices, public information and private knowledge (e.g. inside information).

The model of a strong form of market efficiency has generally been rejected and only used "...as a benchmark against which the importance of deviations from market efficiency can be judged" (Fama 1970, p.414). It has been pointed out by the early example of market making specialists at the New York Stock Exchange. Niederhoffer & Osborne (1966) proved that "insiders" with private knowledge (positions within the order book) are able to gain excessive returns in more than 80% of the undertaken transactions. This contradicts the core idea of a strong-form-effcient market where all information is given and accessible to all investors. However Rozeff & Zaman (1988) provide the scarce counter evidence. They proved in their quantitative study of 679 outsiders and 722 corporate insiders that corporate insiders could not gain excessive returns any different to outsiders.

Regarding the semi-strong form, Fama (1970) states that there is no relevant counter-evidence to reject this hypothesis. This implies that stock prices fully reflect all available information after having them rapidly incorporated and consequently lead to an efficient adjustment. The quantitative "event" study of Fama et al. (1969), using data from the NYSE of 940 stock splits (collected by the CRSP), proves that after the announcement of stock splits (public information) abnormal returns cannot be gained. After a prompt price adjustment at the moment of the announcement (new information) there will not be any further trends and the prices will fluctuate randomly. This confirms the semi-strong hypothesis.

In conclusion, the semi-strong form is the generally accepted pattern of thought, if the meaning of "publicly available" is accurately defined (Jensen 1978). In non-collegiate surroundings this form represents the basic understanding of an efficient market. As possible contradictions to market efficiency have been proven false and explained by scientists, research became as popular as Behavioural Finance and will which will be discussed later.

### *2.2.2 Modern Portfolio Theory (MPT)*

With his pioneering work Markowitz (1952, 1956, 1959) laid the foundation for MPT, for which he was lauded with the Nobel Prize in 1990. His theory is the conceptual framework for portfolio management methods used by practitioners. It is also the groundwork for evolutionary theories of renowned academics including the Single-Index-Model (Sharpe 1963), the Capital Asset Pricing Model (Sharpe 1964, Lintner 1965, Mossin, 1966), and the Arbitrage Pricing Theory (Ross 1976).

Markowitz (1952) explains that the biggest challenge for an investor is to find the perfect combination of stocks ("risky assets") in regards to expected return and variance of return; in other words an efficient portfolio in terms of yield and risk.

#### 2.2.2.1 *Efficient Frontier*

A basic assumption for the perfect combination of stocks is that the portfolio with the highest return is not automatically the portfolio with the lowest risk (variance). This idea assumes that either the expected return of a portfolio increases when the investor is willing to take additional risk or a risk-averse investor is able to reduce the variance in exchange to a lower expected return. Markowitz (1952) defines this connection as the E-V rule (Expected return – Variance of returns). This enables an investor to calculate an infinite number of portfolios allocated out of the world's stock portfolio. As a consequence, this approach also provides a dazzling array in terms of risk and return. Figure 2 highlights that the most efficient portfolios lay on the grey semicircle ("Efficient Frontier") which are "...those with minimum V for given E or more and maximum E for given V or less..." (Markowitz 1952, p.82).

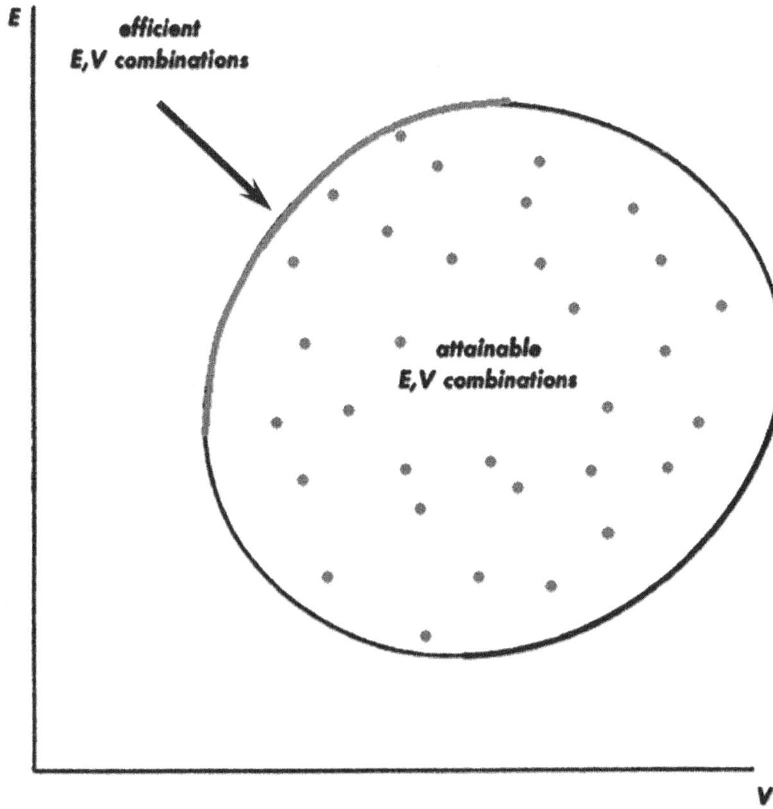


Figure 1: Attainable vs. Efficient Combinations of Risky Assets (adapted from: Roy 1952, 435; Markowitz 1952, p.82; Markowitz 1956, p.111)

Markowitz (1999) states that Roy's article (1952) shows fewer drawbacks than his own as Roy used the standard deviation instead of the variance as his measure of risk. Furthermore, he identifies the potential set of combinations as an envelope curve instead of a circle and anticipated the capital market line (CML) and the "super-efficient portfolio", long before Tobin (1958) and Sharpe (1963) developed their theories.

### 2.2.2.2 *Tobin Separation Theorem*

Markowitz' assumptions (1952, 1956), in particular the use of the criteria expected returns and variance were justified by Tobin (1958), again a of the Nobel Prize laureate. The innovative thinking and core of Tobin's article (Markowitz 1999) is the idea of a portfolio selection model with n risky assets and one risk free asset (cash). Moreover Tobin argues that the market portfolio might be quite inefficient even if all investors hold mean-variance-efficient portfolios. Markowitz (1999) concluded, that the idea of Tobin (1958) was pathbreaking but cautious while Sharpe (1963) revolutionised financial economics. How a riskless asset allows and affects the creation of a "super-efficient" portfolio is illustrated in Figure 3.

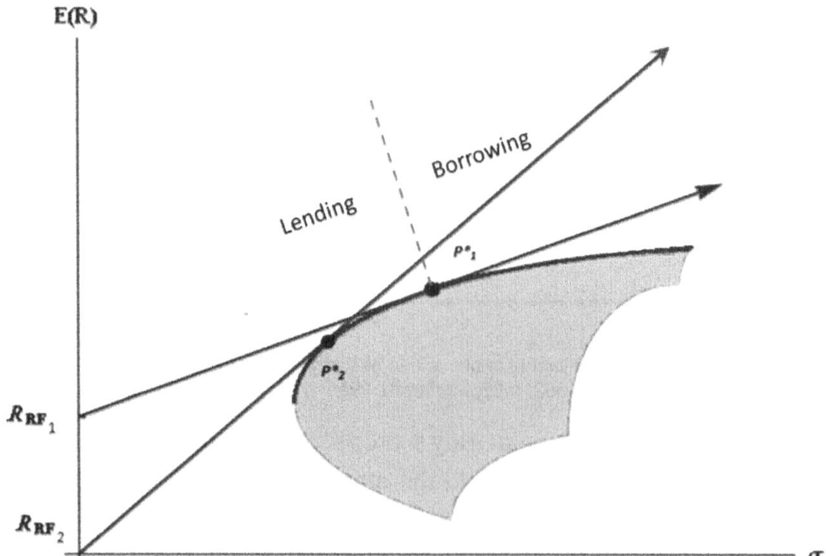


Figure 2: CML, super-efficient portfolio and riskless assets (adapted from: Roy 1952, p.435; Tobin 1958, p.78; Sharpe 1963, p.286; Brealey & Myers 2003, p.193; Fama & French 2004; p.27)

The figure comprises the four fundamental characteristics. While the grey area represents all feasible E-V combinations, the bold curve illustrates the efficient border. The capital market line (CML) starts from the point on the vertical axis at the rates of return on the risk-free assets and tangent to the efficient frontier. RF1 represents the idea of the Sharpe ratio (1963) that Treasury Bills can be regarded as risk-free (standard deviation: 0) and the related line is the capital asset line (CAL). $RF_2$ follows Tobin's (1958) assumption that the return of a risk-free asset is zero. At the point where the lines are tangent to the efficient frontier one will find the super-efficient portfolio as it is the perfect combination of risky and risk-free assets (Fama & French 2004).

Building on this fundamental knowledge Sharpe (1964) developed the security market line (SML). In contrast to the CML and CAL it does not measure risk and return of portfolios (asset combinations) but those of single assets (stocks); hence a combination within a portfolio (Fama & French 2004). Before, this model is described in detail, the next subsection looks at global diversification and the ideal quantity of allocated securities.

#### *2.2.2.3 Diversification*

Markowitz's (1952) E-V rule implies an adequate diversification which depends on the number of securities and on a diversification across sectors and industries in order to reduce variance. In general, companies within the same industry usually show high covariances among themselves as they react "similar" to economic events which leads to a higher risk exposure. Consequently, an investor holds a mean-variance efficient portfolio when a given (individual) level of variance (risk) receives the highest possible expected return (Campbell et al. 1997). Or, like another Nobel Prize winner famously states "Don't put all your eggs in one basket..." (Samuelson 1967, p.1). In order to reduce or even eliminate the unsystematic risk the equity allocation must show a perfect distribution of uncorrelated stocks. The only remaining risk is systematic.

Evans & Archer (1968) conduct one of the first empirical investigations on the question how many stocks should be allocated in a portfolio. They applied a data set of 470 stocks listed in the S&P 500 index in 1958 and used quantitative univariate analysis for the period 01/1958-07/1968. They estimated the level of systematic variation at 0.1166 for the whole portfolio. Further, they conclude a diversification over 10 stocks is enough as the relationship between the level of dispersion and the number of stocks shows a rapidly decreasing function which approximates asymptotically the level of systematic variation. They found proof that most of the unsystematic risk is eliminated after having added the eighth stock to a portfolio. Only big increases lead to a further reduction of risk which was indicated by both t- and F-tests. Even though, this result has been cited throughout following academic literature it also evoked discussions and gained criticism.

Elton & Gruber (1977) criticise that Evans & Archer (1968) employed a simulation approach while advanced statistical models allow a better and analytical expression of the determination of the risk-return relationship for new conditions. They argued that the definition of risk was improper and according to their opinion "...the variation of the expected return on the population of stocks under consideration..." (Elton & Gruber 1977, p.420) would do better. They examined a data set from the NYSE and the American Stock Exchange and used weekly returns of two samples over the time period 6/1971 – 6/1974. Most of their investigations based on the small sample (150 stocks). They validated their findings as they show that the calculated the total variance of return and the expected portfolio variance by using a bigger sample (3,290 securities) had the same characteristics. Their results show a minimum total risk of 7.07 (equally weighted population portfolio) and a maximum risk of 46.811 (single stock portfolios). They conclude that Evans & Archer (1968) were right about the major decrease in risk if 10 uncorrelated stocks are allocated to a portfolio (variance: 11.033) but that it is 156% higher than the minimum. Especially for institutional investors it is quite important to diversify to that point where marginal benefits just exceed marginal costs

(Statman 1987). For Elton & Gruber (1977), reasonable levels of distribution start with portfolios of 28 stocks (20% higher than minimum total risk) but they recommend allocating 110 stocks (5% above minimum risk level).

Statman (1987) confirms the findings of Elton & Gruber (1977). He used a formula like Elton & Gruber (1977) / Markowitz (1959) and an estimate of the risk premium similar to Ibbotson Associates (1985). He applied an equally weighted version of the S&P 500 index while investigating the period 1926-1984. He conducted his study by differentiating between borrowers and lenders and using the Treasury Bill rate as proxy for the lending rate. They estimated an alpha of 2% which is calculated by the Call Money rate (< 2%) plus commissions that brokers normally charge. Though, Statman (1987) also concludes that borrowers need a minimum of 40 stocks to create a healthy diversification.

In contrast to the above mentioned research which solely investigated the US stock market in terms of diversification, first evidence in regards to international diversification was provided by Solnik (1974). He used a similar approach to Evans & Archer's (1968) but applied it to seven European stock markets (Belgium, France, Germany, Italy, Switzerland, The Netherlands, and the United Kingdom). Solnik (1974) finds that an American investor is well-diversified domestically if he allocates 20 stocks. For a further decrease in unsystematic risk of 3% additional investments in 50 more stocks is needed. The remaining risk (27% for the U.S. market) cannot be eliminated by only investing on Wall Street. If the already mentioned 20 stocks are picked from international markets a substantial decrease (> 50%) of systematic or unique risk (above the red line) could be achieved which is graphed in Figure 4 (next page).

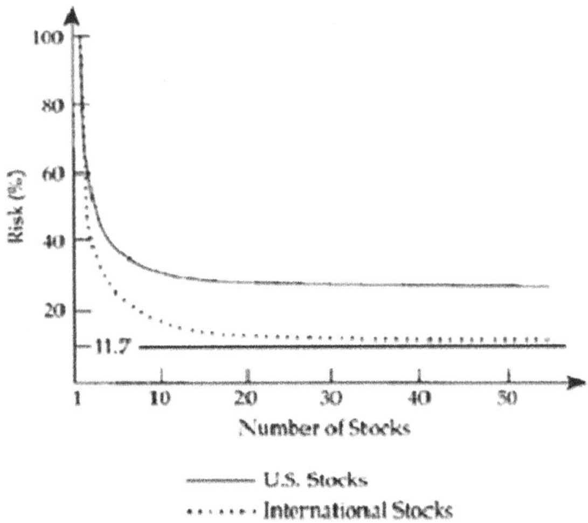


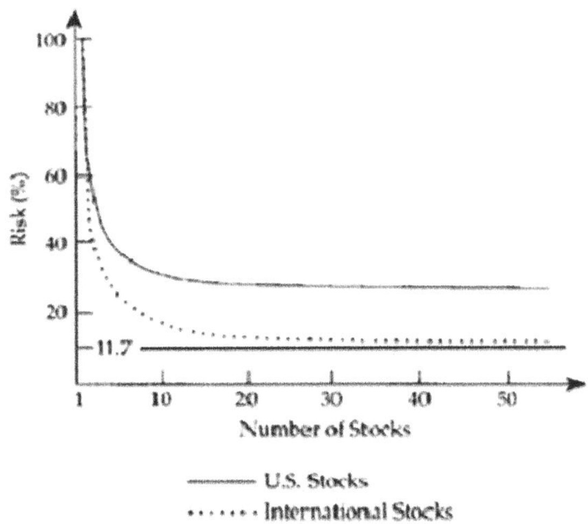


Figure 3: Diversification: International (above) and inter-industrial (below); adapted from: Solnik 1974, p.92; Brealey *et al.* 2009, pp.328-329.

Solnik (1974) calculated the undiversifiable risk of this "international" market at 11.7% (below the red line). Another important result is, that further optimisation is possible, if the international stocks are also diversified across industries, as demonstrated in Figure 4. The results have been and are still so important that their article was reprinted in 1995.

Odien & Solnik (1993) reanalysed if global diversification is still beneficial bearing in mind that nearly 70% of the global market capitalisation is represented by non-U.S securities. They used volatility as a measure of risk. Most importantly, they were the first to take into account the correlations between the single country markets and hence underline the importance to allocate uncorrelated stocks to construct a well-diversified portfolio. Consequently this should also be considered in regards to an international or inter-industry diversification, which plays a pivotal role in this dissertation. Odier & Solnik (1993) picked up the idea of efficient frontier mentioned by Markowitz (1952) and Sharpe (1964) and found that substantial efforts are realised in regard of a really efficient portfolio, as shown in Figure 5 for the decade 1980 to 1990 (U.S. dollar).

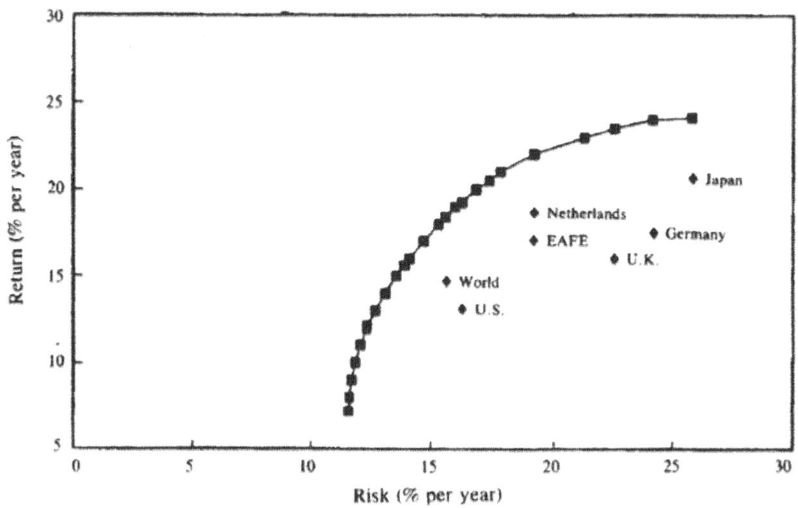


Figure 4: Efficient Frontier for Stocks (Odier & Solnik 1993, p.69)

They suggest that an international portfolio with a return equal to an U.S.-portfolio (13.3% annualised) shows a risk decrease of two thirds.

Inversely, given the risk level (16.2% p.a. for the U.S. stocks) the international allocation (> 19%) outperformed the U.S.-portfolio (16.3%) by around 7% per annum. A major drawback of their study is the lacking of additional inter-sector diversification like in Solnik's (1974) earlier study. However they conclude that 90% of the monthly variation of returns could be explained by the asset allocation and only 10% by stock-picking.

### *2.2.3 Capital Asset Pricing Model (CAPM)*

The major outcome of Sharpe's (1964) theory for which he gained the Nobel Prize is the "securities market line" (SML) which displays the linear dependency between beta (systematic) risk and market return of single assets as it is shown in Figure 6.

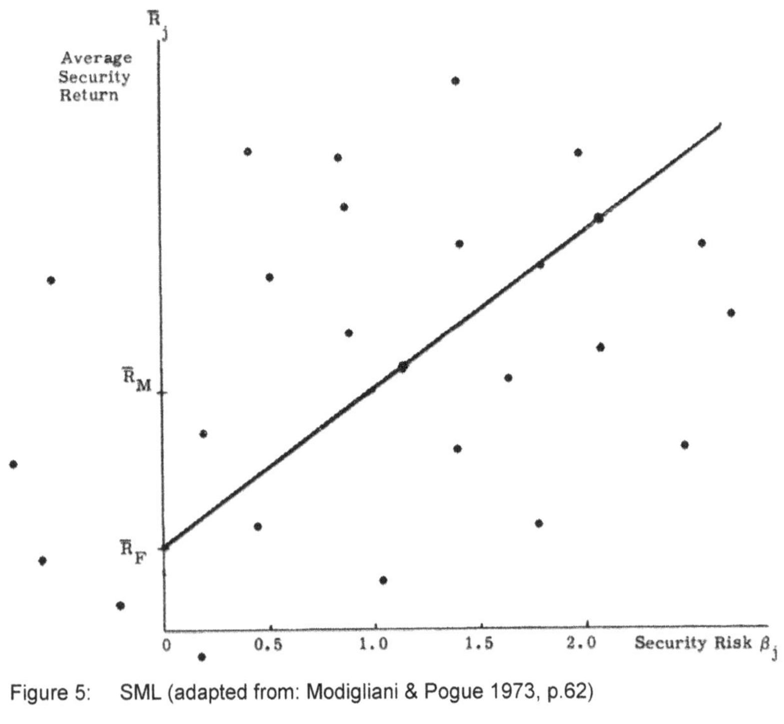


Figure 5: SML (adapted from: Modigliani & Pogue 1973, p.62)

Based on the findings of Markowitz (1952, 1959) and Tobin (1958) the academics extended them to design an equilibrium model of stock prices under risky conditions. Sharpe (1964) was able to show that the risk premium is proportional to the beta. Following the review of Dimson & Mussavian (1998) only Sharpe was lauded with the Nobel Prize as the other major contributors to the contemporary body of thought died to early, like Mossin (1966) and Lintner (1965a,b), or did not even publish their work, like Treynor (1961). As the assumptions and limitations of the CAPM (Black et al. 1972, Sharpe 1964) are widely explained and in most parts equal to those of the EMH and other important theories, they could be recognised as valid and taken for granted even though they might not truly reflect the reality (Brealey & Myers 2003; Brealey *et al.* 2009).

As CAPM investors are expected to hold perfectly diversified portfolios, the unsystematic risk is already eliminated. Consequently, the expected return of a security linearly correlated to its beta risk. The expected return of a single security results from the addition of the risk-free rate and the risk premium of the stock. The latter is calculated by the multiplication of the company's beta with the expected market return minus the risk-free rate. The beta is calculated as the covariance between the rate of return of the single asset and the market portfolio (or a perfect proxy) divided by the variance of the market portfolio (Fama & French 2004; Sharpe 1964). As this is a correct mathematical and logical deduction from the assumptions of the MPT, the CAPM is consequently valid (Spremann 2008). The reliability however depends on the possibility of a deductive empirical observation of testable hypothesis (Popper 1934). In the case of Sharpe's (1964) theory this was not possible until the construction of the CRSP database in the late 1960s (Dimson & Mussavian 1999). The first decisive tests of the CAPM were conducted by Black et al. (1972) followed by a wide range of subsequent discussions and tests (Spremann 2008).

Black et al. (1972) used a sample of 1,952 NYSE listed stocks in the period 01/1926 – 3/1966 for the calculation of stock returns (gathered from CRSP) and chose the 30-day rate on T-bills as the risk-free rate (gathered from Salomon Brothers & Hutzler). Out of this proxy they formed ten portfolios which were reallocated consistently by using an instrumental variable to gain efficiency and eliminate selection bias. The researchers conclude that the relation between beta risk and mean excess return is linear but reject the traditional form of the CAPM as the intercept and the slope of the cross-sectional relation varied with different subperiods (Dimson & Mussavian 1999).

Fama and MacBeth's (1973) methodology was quite similar but they used an improved approach. Their proxy for the market portfolio is slightly bigger than Black et al.'s (1972) as the observation period is enlarged (1/1926-6/1968); however results were similar. They were neither able to reject the hypothesis that investors should consider the linear relationship between the portfolio-risk and expected return nor could they find any other measure of risk (besides the portfolio risk) which orderly affects the mean returns. However they also confirmed that the traditional form of Sharpe's (1964) model shows weak statistical significance. To strengthen statistical significance academics evolved generalisations as summarised below.

Black's (1972) advanced model (Zero-Beta CAPM) does not allow short-selling (borrowing) of the riskless asset. Furthermore, he replaced the riskless asset by a zero-beta portfolio which is per definition uncorrelated with the market portfolio but expected to have the same return. Such a portfolio can be created by the perfect allocation of stock with positive and negative betas balancing the beta to zero. Black's (1972) version, backed by an essay of Rubinstein (1973), accounts for some evidence against the traditional version of Sharpe (1964) where the zero-beta portfolio showed a higher estimated mean return than the risk-free asset (Campbell *et al.* 1997). A second advancement was created by Brennan

(1971) which allows lending and short-selling but at different rates of interest and therefore limits the zero-beta rate to the spread. Both of these advancements were important as they better reflect the capital markets' reality. It is obvious that the credit interest, which an investor earns for his secure investment, is lower than the debit risk he has to pay for credits.

Merton (1969, 1971, and 1973), also a Nobel Prize laureate, extended the CAPM to multiple periods and gave it a continuous-time formulation which became the Intertemporal Capital Asset Pricing Model (ICAPM). Further efforts to improve the traditional Model like the static C-CAPM (consumption-based) by Rubinstein (1976), Lukas (1978) and Breeden (1979) and the non-static extension (conditional C-CAPM) were made by Hansen & Richard (1987). Even though the power of the first model was weak due to empirical evidence and testing of the conditional C-CAPM is difficult (Spremann 2008), the ideas encroached on the considerations of other fields of study like Behavioral Finance.

Not least due to these advancements practitioners interpreted the ambiguousness of and about the model as follows: the CAPM is not only theoretically correct it is also a sound paradigm from the empirical point of view. Even today, the evaluation of companies and specifically the costs of capital are regularly determined with the CAPM (Spremann 2008).

#### *2.2.3.1 Roll's Critique*

Ambiguity was the background for Roll's (1977) categorical criticism towards all empirical tests of the CAPM. He mentions that even if the proxy of market portfolio is perfect (index with all securities of the world weighted by their capitalisation) it does not reflect the correct weighting of all investments of all people (Spremann 2008). Roll (1977) argues that the rejection and the empirical validation of the CAPM can therefore generate no perception at all. The most crucial mistake is made, if a false index is used as a proxy which misleads to a validation of the CAPM. This happens in two out of three situations of inconsistencies within tests as outlined in Table 1.

Table 1: Summary of CAPM research adapted from Spremann (2008, p.316)

| Situation | Issue | Consequences |
|---|---|---|
| 1 | Divergence between index used in the empirical investigation and the perfect security market index | Design of a perfect proxy and reiteration of the tests |
| 2 | The real Investment-Opportunity-Set (IOS) has a much broader scope than the capital market | Further testing is not reasonable as the MPT is a quite general theory which could explain events on the capital market only in parts as most investments are made apart from market actions. |
| 3 | The IOS basically is consistent with the capital market but investors do not adhere to the MPT,... | Consequences are to the situations 3a and 3b |
| 3a | ...because of limited rational behaviour (further discussed in the Behavioural Finance chapter) | For descriptive purposes models are required which could picture the constrict rationality |
| 3b | ...because they acknowledge the MPT a good but to simple theory which has to be enlarged (further discussed in the chapter of multi-factor models) | As investors show superrational behaviour the MPT should be used as a basis for further development |

According to Spremann (2008) researchers argued that Roll's critique is generally correct and that the influence of real estate and human capital is of great importance to the decisions of private investors but not such much for institutional investors. The major aim of subsequent studies and tests was to find out if those institutionals behave like rational investors in regards to the MPT. They tried to mitigate the problems detected in situation 1 by using perfect indices and to improve the power of their tests. This led to the detection of anomalies which stand in contrast to the CAPM. As Schwert (2003) states, most of the anomalies are not facts but temporary phenomena. According to Black (1993) they generally disappear soon after their manifestation. However, an anomaly may survive if it is combined with an additional risk which is not captured by the beta and the CAPM.

Fama and French's issued in their article (1992) about the anomalies of size and book-to-market equity a statement which opened the discussion on whether asset-pricing might be irrational. From here science branched in two directions (Spremann 2008). The first one builds on the traditional theory, that the CAPM is not wrong but it was weak for some periods (Black 1993, Spremann 2008). As a result the rational investors do not follow the MPT precisely and the traditional single-factor model of Sharpe (1964) has been widened to multi-factor models which dramatically improved its reliability of the correlation between risk and return. The second direction leads to the area of Behavioural Finance where the investor is not completely rational. The anomalies and their coherence with behaviouristic approaches are discussed in the next chapter.

#### *2.2.3.2 Anomalies & Behavioral Finance*

Fama (1998), an advocate of the EMH, states that most anomalies are not able to dismiss the idea of market efficiency. Nevertheless, he confirms that some anomaly findings passed robustness tests. Most of the anomalies seem to be fragile and disappear when they are measure in another way. As he expected, further studies in this area were consequently undertaken and therefore missing out this kind of research would be an unforgiveable sacrilege.

Shiller (2003) seized this suggestion in his extensive survey and concludes that Fama's (1964) criticism was weak. Even though the theory of market efficiency pictures an ideal world it is not able to describe real markets whereas exponents of the behavioural finance movement do explain the origins of "anomalies" like speculative bubbles, booms, or crashes.

Kahneman & Tversky's "Prospect Theory" (1979), for which Kahneman received the Nobel Prize, proposes, contrary to the then accepted opinion of the strict "rational choice model" (*Homo oeconomicus)* a framework in which rationality was replaced by findings on judgement heuristics and cognitive biases (Tversky & Kahneman 1974). Based on this theory, Behavioral Finance contributes to a far-ranging improvement in the understanding of the participants and their decisions, affecting prices and returns as summarised by Baltussen (2008) in his Ph.D.-thesis. He concluded that a better understanding of market behaviour can be achieved by applying the findings of psychological and sociological sciences. In order to emphasize the major drawbacks of the EMH and the CAPM, the best-known and painstakingly investigated examples of behavioural patterns (Shiller 2003), known as the "effects" of **momentum** and **long-time reversal** will now be discussed.

#### *2.2.3.3 Long-time Reversal Effect*

DeBondt & Thaler (1985), using a data sample of CRSP ranging over a period of 56 years (1926-1982), observed, that "winners" (stocks in top decile over three years regarding their return) were prone to demonstrate negative accrued returns in the subsequent three years while "losers" (stocks in the bottom decile) behave vice versa. Picking up the findings of Kahneman *et al.* (1982) that an average investor overweights latest news events and undervalues previous information, their empirical results from analysing NYSE common stocks, showss that former "losers" outperformed the market by 19.6% on average while former "winners" underperformed by 5% ($\Delta$ = 24.6%). They also proved Graham (1959) right with his thesis that an undervaluation needs 1.5 to 2.5 years before it recovers. A third important outcome was that the loser portfolios have significantly lower betas in average than the winners which makes them simultaneously less risky and more profitable.

Further evidence was given by Vermaelen & Verstringe (1986) for the Belgian market; they recovered the same reversal effect operating with a similar methodology. De Bondt & Thaler (1987) reinforced their assertion in their follow-up paper. Lakonishok *et al.* (1994) empirically analysed a broad universe (all NYSE & AMEX stocks) within a 28 years period, using enhanced data sources regarding firm size information to mitigate survivorship and selection bias. Further they picked up on the criticism of Chan (1986, 1987) about the reversal effect deriving from changes in beta-risk and on the assumptions of Keim (1983) and Reinganum (1983) that it is primarily a size effect which was uncovered by Banz (1981). The latter one is eliminated by trading or by the possibility that in previous studies survivorship bias (e.g. data snooping) did the trick for similar results (Malkiel 2003, Schwert 2003); it therefore will not be discussed furthermore. However, the long-term reversal effect endured and as in subsequent periods prices fluctuate randomly this anomaly does not imply market inefficiency as Fluck *et al.* (1997) prove within their simulation. Even after the bust of the dot.com bubble in March 2000, Youssef *et al.* (2010) give evidence that this contrarian effect still exists. In summary, building trading models upon the long-term reversal effect does not stand in contrast to the CAPM (Spremann 2008).

#### *2.2.3.4 Momentum Effect*

Campbell et al. (1997) as well as Kent & Titman (1997) suggest that stock prices tend to follow the same direction for six to 12 months before they reverse themselves. This section will deal with the findings of Jegadeesh & Titman (1993), generally known by the colloquial Wall Street adage "the trend is your friend" (Spremann 2008, p.320). By having analysed NYSE and AMEX stocks (CRSP data) over a time period of 35 years (1965-1989) the researchers found that portfolios based on relative strength trading strategies (sell losers - buy winners) show average excess returns of more than 12%, once those stocks which recorded the best performance over the past six months are bought and held for the subsequent half-year period. Already Levy (1967) suggests that strategies based on past relative strength will outperform the market and some institutional investors followed his approach like mutual funds (Grinblatt & Titman 1989).

### 2.2.3.5 *Value and B/M-stocks vs. Glamour Stocks*

In contrast to the effects above which are associated with irrational behaviours of investors, Fama & French (1992) question the rationality topic but prove the relation between beta and average return to be weak during the 1941-1990 period. This is contradictory to their investigation in 1973 (time period 1/1926-6/1968) of all NYSE listed stocks (max: 1,261 securities; database: CRSP) where they supported the implications of Sharpe's two-parameter model. In the recent test, Fama & French (1992) state that the average return shows only a weak positive relation to their betas when analysing an extended data sample from 6/1963 to 12/1990,and using a well-thought-out test approach (Spremann 2008). They analysed the CRSP-data (returns), covering all stocks (excluding financial firms) from the NYSE, AMEX and after 1973 also from the NASDAQ and merged COMPUSTAT-data (income statement and balance sheet). Similar to Fama & MacBeth (1973) they used the cross-sectional regression approach for their asset-pricing tests. Fama & French (1992) proved that the traditional CAPM does not show the demanded linearity of beta and risk premium (return) and that the (big) institutional price- and market-dominating investors adhere to the MPT (situation 3). They concluded in this outstanding article (best in "The Journal of Finance" in 1992 – Smith-Breeden Prize) that the two variables of size and book-to-market equity can describe the cross-section of stock returns better than beta but it is not possible to predict expected returns, especially for book-to-market-equity. In the next sections alternative models of asset pricing will be mentioned which take account for different risks.

### 2.2.4 *Arbitrage Pricing Theory (APT)*

While the CAPM analyses how investors arrange efficient portfolios the Ross' APT (1976) assumes that a stock's return depends on two sources of risk, macroeconomic "factors" and "noise" (unique events which affect only a certain company). The theory does not define those factors in detail and so the model could be used to include different factors like the oil price, interest rates or the return of the market portfolio (Brealey & Myers 2003). The APT unerringly derives from Markowitz's (1952) MPT as Ross (1976) states that noise terms become negligible through diversification and are ignored when making an investment. Owning a perfectly diversified portfolio the respected risk premium is only affected by pervasive macroeconomic risk ("factors"). Hence, the APT has two things in common with the CAPM. First, unique risk is diversifiable and does not play any role in investment decisions. Second, macroeconomic influences represent certain stock portfolios which are subject to a general factor. If each of these portfolios show an expected risk premium proportional to the portfolio's market risk, only then the CAPM and the APT will lead to the same outcome. A major advantage of this model is that the market portfolio may be one of the "factors" but it does not necessarily has to be (Huberman & Wang 2005). The major drawback is that factors are not specified in contrast to the CAPM which combines all macroeconomic risks in one single factor.

The academics disagree on how many and which factors influence stock prices (Brealey & Myers 2003). Some, like Elton *et al.* (1994) identified six factors including market return as the other five factors (Yield spread, Interest rate, Exchange rate, Real GNP, Inflation) are not able to explain all of influences on cash flows or discount rates. Others, like Roll & Ross (1980), found three to four factors would be enough after having investigated 1,260 American (New York and American Stock Exchanges) stocks during the 1962-1972 period (CRSP data). A third group gives evidence that the number of factors increases with the number of evaluated stocks. Dhrymes *et al.* 1984 conclude in their empirical examination, using a slightly adjusted version of Roll & Ross' (1980) data sample, that only two factors are enough if 15 stocks are evaluated while nine factors are needed for ninety stocks. This indecisive evidence lead to the result that the model has not been adapted by many investors. Furthermore, according to Brealey *et al.* (2009), the complicated use of the APT drives most institutionals to use the CAPM or a static multi-factor model like Fama and French's (1993) as discussed next.

### *2.2.5 Three-factor model (Fama & French)*

Fama & French (1993, 1995) build their "three-factor model" on the findings of their 1992 article. In addition to the CAPM and in contrast to Roll (1976) they used three static factors: market, size and book-to-market and therefore considered the anomalies. While the market factor explains the outperforming stocks in regards to T-Bills, the other factors explain the different returns of stocks. According to Brealey & Myers (2003) the application of the three-factor model is exactly the same as using the APT to estimate the expected returns. Consequently the sensitivity of the different industry groups has to be estimated, because companies of the same industry face the same risks. Some stocks are more sensitive to fluctuations in the returns on the three factors than others but they can be grouped into sectors (Fama & French 1997).

A number of academics examined different markets to test whether the three-factor model outperformed the CAPM. The results were ambiguous as some confirmed the findings of Fama and French (1993) whereas others preferred the CAPM. The supporters Connor & Sehgal (2001) and in parts Nartea *et al.* (2009) examined single developing stock markets (Connor & Sehgal 2001: India; Nartea *et al.* 2009: New Zealand) which therefore might be seen as a weak proxy for the market portfolio. Connor & Sehgal (2001) examined 364 companies from CRISIL-500 index (constructed along the lines of the S&P 500) while the whole market consisted of over 8,000 listed companies (90% are thinly traded) at that point of time. They gathered share data for the 6/1989-3/1999 period from Capital Market Line, a trustworthy database used by Indian practitioners and researchers. The risk-free yield was defined by the 91-day

Treasury Bills which can only be seen as a good proxy for the period 1993-1999 as it the yield was fixed before through governmental regulations. Connor & Sehgal (2001) therefore confirmed the factors of size and market but reject the book-to-market equity factor for the Indian market.

In summary, it could be stated that multi-factor models provide an interesting alternative to the CAPM but as its usefulness is not fully known until new unbiased data is available to provide a true performance check, practitioners will adhere on the traditional models building on the CAPM (Campbell *et al.* 1997).

## 2.3 Recent Developments

Recently, two major developments can be observed. First, there has been interesting changes regarding market efficiency caused by increasing share turnovers, the so-called high-frequency traders and the effects of the work of financial analysts and Investor Relations departments. Second, the beginning of international cross-industry investigations presents new interesting insights regarding the validity of the CAPM.

### *2.3.1 Three-factor model (Fama & French)*

Recently, Chordia et al. (2011) suggest by using variance ratio tests on Trade & Quote (TAQ) data of NYSE listed stocks in the 1993-2008 period (CRSP database), that intraday volatility decreased and therefore, stock prices behave more closely to the random walk. This is foremost driven by an increased trading frequency and smaller trade sizes which result from lowered transaction costs and the widespread use of quantitative trading strategies as the researchers explain their findings. As it was the second investigation of this kind, this study validated the findings of Chordia et al. (2008) where they also stated, that changes in market efficiency in the direction of the strong form exist, even though that these changes are driven by stock price information and not corporate-communicated information.

These findings are supported by the large sample study of Chung & Hrazdil (2010) who analysed 4,222 NYSE stocks during a 10-year period (1993-2002). By using multiple regressions they found that the increased market efficiency is driven by higher turnovers (through arbitrage activities) and the more effective incorporation of new information into the stock prices.

### *2.3.2 Investor Relations and Financial Analysts*

Although a trend exists in the direction towards a strong-efficient market, this is currently not the case yet for most of the international stock markets (Popović 2004). The existence of the strong form would eliminate the raison d'être of financial (share) analysts and investor relation activities. On the contrary activities like "delegated monitoring" still help to increase the market's efficiency (Popović 2004) by providing with valuation relevant information (Pietzsch 2004).

### *2.3.3 International Aspects*

As in subsequent studies Fama & French's (1992) approach was defined as unconditional and criticised for its inherent joint hypothesis (e.g. Pettengill *et al.* 1995, Elsas *et al.* 2003). Hence, Pettengill *et al.* (1995) and other opponents of Fama & French's approach created a conditional beta test (CBT) which has been used in most studies since the mid-1990s, because it allowed a separate and independent testing of the CAPM. Within these studies, where different stock markets were examined a significant relationship between beta risk and return could be testified (Pettengill *et al.* (US: 1995), Isakov (Switzerland: 1999), Fraser *et al.* (UK: 2003), Elsas *et al.* (Germany: 2003) and Ho *et al.* (Hong Kong: 2006)).

Most of the deductive studies were limited to single stock markets and did not use the global market. Even though they contributed substantially to the contemporary body of thought, this might be the wrong proxy for the market portfolio. For example a huge number of studies support the CAPM in general, but big differences can be recognised regarding the significance of the positive relationship (Freeman & Guermat 2006) which derive from special characteristics of each single stock market. This drawback might be wiped out by an international investigation. Fletcher (2000) and Tang & Shum (2003) who both used the CBT approach examined the risk-return relation of different countries simultaneously (Fletcher: 18 in USD; Tang & Shum: 13 in domestic currencies) against the World Market (Fletcher: MSCI World Index; Tang & Shum: MSCI World Index plus an equally weighted World Index) by using data of the major indices instead of single stocks. Both studies show countries in which an investment is more profitable than an investment in the World Market itself.

### *2.3.4 Sector Specifics*

The research regarding sector specifics is scarce. Only the quantitative study of Mergner & Bulla (2008) gives valid international evidence that huge differences between sectors exist (**beta**: Food & Beverages 0.65 vs. Technology 1.49; **excess return per week**: Automobiles & Parts: 0.02%; Healthcare: 0.17%). Furthermore, their research proxy is quite near to reality as they use a pan-european sample of 600 stocks and 18 supersectors. This is one of the largest samples in recent literature.

## 2.4 Gaps in knowledge and literature

As it becomes obvious international and intersectoral research is still in its infancy. Even though first moves are made, as mentioned in last two sections, there is hardly any evidence about emerging and developing markets. Furthermore, the interaction of markets analogue to their comparative advantages has to be further illuminated as they are strongly connected to sector-specifics. Furthermore, by the use of more comprehensive data a reassessment of the preferability of the various asset-pricing models could be conducted.

# Chapter 3: Research Methodology

## 3.1 Chapter Introduction

Within this chapter the scientific approach of this dissertation is discussed. The processes and methods are described to obtain valid and reliable results from the undertaken studies as presented in Chapter 4. This practical method is supported by descriptive statistics to analyse the data.

## 3.2 Preconceptions

Fundamental knowledge about the EMH, the MPT, the CAPM and the aforementioned stock market anomalies was gathered from finance courses at Bachelor's and Master's level. In addition, the author looks back on a profound professional stock market experience as he is a broker and asset manager at the Stuttgart Stock Exchange; hence, the knowledge is not only theoretical. Having been tasked with the reconstruction of the equity portfolio based on actual and accepted knowledge this work follows a scientific approach which is not affected by the author's own preconceptions. Therefore a quantitative research strategy is followed throughout this dissertation to rely on hard, objective evidence.

Even though the drawbacks of the EMH, MPT and CAPM theories have been widely discussed within courses and academic literature, the interest to undertake wide-ranging research studies on the cross-section of stock returns raised due to criticism based on weak proxies for the global stock market. This gives a deep insight on whether the CAPM is still able to explain the cross-section of stock return or if it is dead. Before the scientific approach of this work is explained in detail, a close look is given how relevant literature was found and why the author is able to guarantee the highest quality standard of the reviewed articles. This is of vast importance in order to approach this controversy topic adequately.

## 3.3 Literature Search

Relevant literature could be gathered from the classic catalogue of the Edinburgh Napier University libraries for fundamental textbooks and the online databases of e-journals and articles which are provided by NU-INlink. Especially, the latter source provides a huge amount of peer-reviewed academic articles summarised by established databases like ScienceDirect (Elsevier), JSTOR Business, Wiley Online Library and Emerald Journals. To find relevant articles the search functions of these databases were used to look for keywords, phrases and authors. Furthermore, the references and quotations of the articles where used to find additional relevant literature to widen the knowledge about the theories and the critiques. All articles were subject to a quality test conducted by the help of the Academic Journal Quality Guide provided by the ABS (Association of Business Schools). Most of the journals referenced in this work are graded with 4 by the ABS Guide which means they publish the most original and best executed research. More than a third of the referenced articles derive from journals with a 4* grade, the so-called World Elite Journals or superscripts. Some regions of the world's stock market have so far not been investigated deeply, hence literature is only little, mostly regional and not up to such a high standard but never below a level of 3 which is still remarkable.

## 3.4 Research Philosophy and Scientific Approach

Bettner *et al.* (1994) state the following threads to reviewed theories in finance: ontology, epistemology, human nature, and methodology. According to Ardalan (2003) most of the finance researchers are functionalists and therefore it is an appropriate paradigm when positivistic methods are used to empirically test the validty of asset-pricing models. By applying such approach (Bryman & Bell 2007), this dissertation observes the World Stock market and verifies and tests the research questions which derive from the theory build up on the empiricism of Sharpe (1964). An extensive analysis is provided following a quantitative strategy. Moreover, it is tested by a two-step cross- sectional analysis if and how the current economic crisis in Japan which followed the ecological disasters shows influences on the allocation and the validity of the theories.

### *3.4.1 Positivism vs. Interpretivism*

To describe what kind of knowledge can be regarded as valid, true and acceptable epistemology offers an appropriate concept originally found in natural sciences. The two major perspectives of epistemology are interpretivism and positivism.

This dissertation uses the positivistic view. An advocate of positivism applies methods from natural sciences to social reality and far beyond. Even though a number of authors are unsure about the constituent elements, Bryman & Bell (2007) describe five widely accepted principles which entail positivism, as presented and described in the table below.

Table 2: The Five Principles of Positivism adapted from Bryman & Bell (2007, p.16.)

| Principle | Explanation |
|---|---|
| 1. Phenomenalism | Phenomena and knowledge validated by the senses can be warranted as knowledge |
| 2. Deductivism | The aim of theory is to create hypotheses which can be tested with observations or data and allow an explanation of laws to be assessed |
| 3. Inductivism | The collection of facts (data or observations) builds the foundation for laws to gain knowledge |
| 4. Impartiality | Science must be undertaken in a value free and therefore objective way |
| 5. Differentiation | There must be a clear differentiation between normative and scientific statements and the belief that the latter are the true domain of the academic |

In contrast to positivism the other epistemological view is interpretivism and subsumes the critique of writers who questioned whether the scientific model can be successful applied to social science. While positivists try to explain human behaviour the focus of interpretivism lays on the understanding and interpretation of human actions (Weber 1947; Bryman & Bell 2007). This does not seem to be appropriate for research undertaken in finance as even in the field of Behavioural Finance mostly positivistic viewpoints are chosen and most of the academics explain human behaviour.

### *3.4.2 Objectivism vs. Constructivism*

According to Bryman & Bell (2007) one can differentiate between two ontological positions: objectivism and constructivism. The best way to illustrate the difference of these positions is to look at organisation (tangible object) and culture.

From the viewpoint of an objectivist an organisation comes with rules, procedures, mission statements and a hierarchy and is independent from social actors and cannot be influenced by them. Furthermore, the organisation itself exerts pressure on its members so that they follow the given rules and procedures. This can easily be transferred to culture. To function as a full member they have to adopt and internalise widely shared beliefs, roles and customs to be able to socialise themselves (Bryman & Bell 2007). This being the case social entities can be regarded as objective entities with a reality external to social actors. Bringing this in context with the research area of this dissertation it is possible to identify the World Stock Market and the associated asset-pricing models as such organisations because the huge amount of orders and borders have to be followed and noticed by the market participants and investors. Restrictions like trading hours, clearing and settlement regulations and trading habits in general must be adhered as well as methods for the evaluation of stocks and companies like DCF and EVA to name only a few in contexts with the CAPM theory. If a true asset-pricing model exists, which is able to explain the cross-sectional variation of stock returns, an objectivist may derive rules explaining the cross-section most appropriate and hence is able to build a causal and efficient allocation.

In contrast to this constructivism challenges the suggestion that culture and organisation are pre-given and therefore not susceptible to manipulation. Even though renowned supporters argue that constructivism cannot be pushed to the extreme were social actors are able to influence, affect or even create organisations and culture to a very high degree, this dissertation cannot take this position. As the CAPM has very strict rules and regulations, which is also true for the global stock markets in general, it is not possible to even follow the moderate type of constructivism which implies that culture acts as a reference point in a constant process of change and therefore cannot be regarded as an objective reality (Bryman & Bell 2007). For this dissertation the position of objectivism is appropriate as the investors and participants are affected by the stock markets and their inherent rules and orders.

Having discussed and worked out the research philosophies followed within this dissertation (functionalist, positivist, and objectivist) the research approach will be highlighted in the next section.

## 3.5 Research Approach, Strategy and Time Horizon

### *3.5.1 Deductivism vs. Inductivism*

There are two ways to use data in empirical research studies. Either data is used to test a theory which is known as deductive research or to build a theory by using empirical data which is known as inductive research. These approaches describe the relation between research and theory and are of significant importance in regards to the research process.

Advocates of the inductive approach state that social phenomena cannot be explained unless they are based on experience and observations. They argue that theories which develop out of systematic inductive empiricism fit the data better. A second rationale articulated by the supporters of induction arises from the critique on assumptions embraced by the positivistic philosophy. In addition, the EMH, the MPT and the CAPM are existing theories which should be tested in a deductive way. For these reasons the use of an inductive approach is not appropriate for this dissertation. The same can be said about the iterative approach, a mix of deduction and induction, where collected data needs to be further analysed with more data or theory than already considered (Bryman & Bell 2007). This is not the case for the research area covered within this dissertation.

This study will follow the deductive approach where hypotheses are built on existing theories which are then tested empirically, either confirming or rejecting the hypotheses.

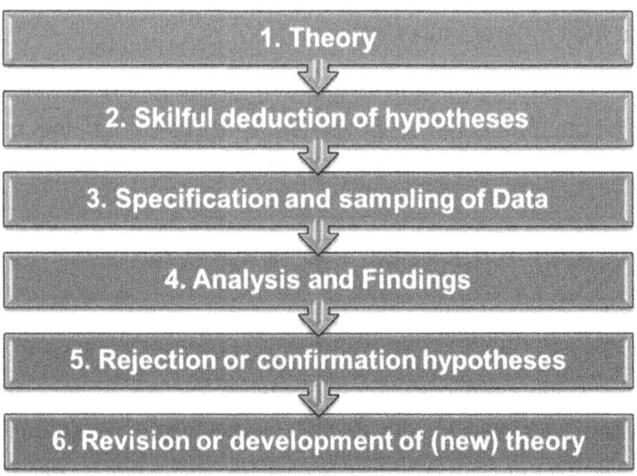


Figure 6: Deduction Process adapted from Bryman & Bell (2007, p.11)

Rejecting is followed by a revision or a completely new theory. This process of deduction is illustrated in figure 7. Most of the academic works in finance are done by deductive studies as it is the more appropriate way to build or enhance theory. It furthermore offers the most common view on the relation between research and theory. As the theories studied to build the foundation of this work are the widely accepted in finance it does not only seem appropriate to take the deductive way; the application of this approach in this dissertation is rather a requisite must.

### *3.5.2 Quantitative vs. Qualitative Research Strategy*

The outcomes of the areas discussed above - epistemological and ontological considerations as well as the connection between research and theory – form two possible research strategies which give a general orientation about the question on how research should be conducted (Saunders *et al.* 2007).

A qualitative strategy should be used if the researcher follows an inductive approach to generate his theory. Furthermore, it is the appropriate way for interpretivists and constructivists who emphasise words in the collection and analysis of data.

In this dissertation the quantitative research strategy is used as it is the common method in finance because it places emphasis on quantification rather than words in the collection and analysis of data. Thus, a quantitative analysis is the only valid and reliable way to create a portfolio showing a perfect allocation of sectors and a worldwide diversification. According to Bryman & Bell (2007), this strategy is appropriate for and should be used by researchers who follow a deductive approach and share a positivistic and objectivistic perspective which is the case for this work.

### 3.5.3 *Cross-sectional vs. Longitudinal*

The time horizon of research activities and therefore its design is often associated with the research strategy and has itself a big impact on how research can be evaluated in terms of reliability, replication and validity. While a longitudinal time horizon could make sense in qualitative and quantitative strategies, a cross-sectional approach typically is used with a quantitative strategy. A combination of quantitative and cross-sectional approaches is employed when unstructured or semi-structured interviews with only a small number of people are conducted. The major advantages for a cross-sectional approach are due to the fact that risks of businesses are changing over time. Thus, a longitudinal method is not appropriate to structure a portfolio reflecting the current market, sector and company situation. Furthermore, the cross-sectional approach is appropriate for an observation of the total market for which this dissertation uses a comprehensive and useful proxy. In addition, this work comprises a repeated investigation to figure out time-variation and to enhance the knowledge about economic influences.

## 3.6 Reliability, Validity and Generalisibility

### 3.6.1 *Reliability*

The raw data, Bloomberg and STOXX uses, is taken from automatically generated records of World's stock exchanges. Inter-rater reliability is given, because the results will not depend on the measurements of this work; anybody can gain these results, if the same methods are used. Test-retest reliability can partly be assumed, because the results are reproducible at any time. As it is a cross-sectional examination they will probably show a new status quo, which is important for portfolio managers to restructure their asset allocation. An inter-method reliability can also be assumed as different types of triangulation are used. Data triangulation is given through a double market investigation while the use of different methods provides a methodological triangulation. In addition, an interaction between observer and subject (here: efficient stock market) does not exist, thus this methods can be seen as reliable.

### *3.6.2 Validity*

Regarding the external validity, generalizability and transferability can be assumed. Transferability can be implied, as studies, which focus on different single international stock markets have adopted a similar approach and gained results akin to those of the pilot. Following the CAPM theory, the beta-return relation applies to the entire financial market. Generalizability can be implied because the developing markets were excluded from the observation due to the fact that these yet cannot be recognised as efficient.

In regard to internal validity, face validity can be assumed, because an investment with an inherent high risk should be paid off with a higher return and not every stock will stand on the SML. Content validity is given, because academics support the idea of turning the construct of the CAPM into a reasonable test by focussing on its main drivers, beta and return. Construct validity can be assured as the approach directly refers to the prized theory and its widely accepted conditional interpretation.

## 3.7 Practical Method

### *3.7.1 Data Sampling*

The sample is collected from secondary data by using the STOXX Global 1800, an ex-ante efficient stock index which has been created for analytical issues by STOXX Ltd, a renowned index issuer. This is convenient, because the data especially constructed for valid and reliable results is free from biases as the sample derives from historic data that can no longer be influenced. Discussing the representativeness of this index, the statement of an all-embracing investigation has to be relativized at this point. Even though the data sample consists of 1,800 stocks representing 19 supersectors from 24 countries there are nonetheless some limitations to the representative subset. The research is limited to the most developed stock markets and only those companies are taken into consideration which shares belong to the most liquid within the international market (transactions) and which market capitalisation is under the top 600 in their region (America, Europe, Asia/Pacific). To overcome these limitations is essential for the overall aim to support portfolio managers by providing them with results they can apply in daily business. They will not invest in illiquid stocks of undeveloped markets and therefore the limitations are crucial.

Stock returns as well as the required raw beta for each stock in relation to the STOXX Global 1800 index were obtained from a Bloomberg terminal. In order to create a mid-to-long-term portfolio the returns and the raw betas of each stock are calculated on the basis of the past 360 days. For various reasons (e.g. momentum effect, reversal effect, triangulation, etc.) the data sampling was conducted twice, first in November 2010 and second in April 2011. As there have been changes in the index formation the data had to be modified (over 25 stocks have changed). Furthermore, all calculations were done under the limitation of an equally weighted index or allocation due to the fact that weightings are changing as well as the formation itself which would entail in different types of biases.

### *3.7.2 Procedure*

#### *3.7.2.1 Information retrieval*

Different suppliers (secondary data) provide the required statistical information. The type of information derives from the research questions itself. First, the name (ISIN) of all stocks within the STOXX Global 1800 is required. To figure out the stocks with the best risk-return relation the betas and received returns of each of the 1,800 stocks is needed. To give a statement about the specific character of a supersector the information about its composition is required. In addition, information about the companies' locations is necessary to show differences between country specific economic risks.

#### *3.7.2.2 Piloting*

A pilot experiment was conducted to test the feasibility and the design of this research approach. Within this small scale preliminary study (which was part within the Research Proposal) the global Automobile & Parts sector (October 2010: 47 components) was examined by using data which complied with the required information.

The pilot answered the question where and how the information was gathered. and how it was transferred in an Excel spread sheet were it was fitted with an add-on to fulfil the requirements of the Bloomberg software. The spread sheet was linked to Bloomberg which assigned betas and total return measures to each of the stocks. To provide both valid and reliable results descriptive statistical methods were used throughout the analysis.

### *3.7.3 Statistical Methods*

The basis for the quantitative analysis of data is the combination of simple graphics and descriptive analysis which provides a summary of the sample and the measures. As it is common to focus on three characteristics in an univariate analysis, in Chapter 4 the central tendency, the dispersion and the distribution give first insight in the examination of the World Stock market by looking on the study variables of beta and return. Furthermore, the statistical dependence is examined by using correlation and regression analysis between those variables. In particular, it is analysed if differences between supersectors exist and if the location has an impact on those variables by using mathematical and statistical methods (see Appendices 1 and 2). As these methods can be seen as valid and reliable, in the next subsection issues are discussed in order to avoid biases that could derive from or ethical aspects.

## 3.8 Ethical Issues

Only little contact points exist between the research and ethical aspects as (raw) secondary data from trustable resources and providers is used. Furthermore, the quantitative analysis is carried out without manipulating the given data. The dissertation is barred from personal, selection and commercial biases and hence all unethical practices connected to humans will not appear. To avoid plagiarism the work is written on the author's own and others authors' work cited.

# Chapter 4: Analysis & Discussion

## 4.1 Chapter Introduction

This part of the dissertation provides the major results of the empirical analysis and the implications of those findings. It is illustrated how the statistical test and analysis were conducted on the data before the findings are presented and discussed. The structure of this chapter follows the research questions and addresses one after another.

## 4.2 Structure of the analysis

This section informs about how the analysis is generally conducted. First, the proxy for the World Market is explained by giving a short summary of the examined stock universe which can be taken from the table below. As the analysis was carried out twice, all measures and information are provided for both dates – November 2010 and April 2011. Secondly, descriptive statistics are used to give detailed information about beta and return from different viewpoints: for the whole proxy and for each supersector and country. Thirdly, the relation between beta and return is analysed by utilising correlations and regressions. Finally, a logical and causal model of asset allocation is built on those findings.

## 4.3 Proxy analysis

Figure 8 visualises the market formation in proportion to the 24 countries. In this

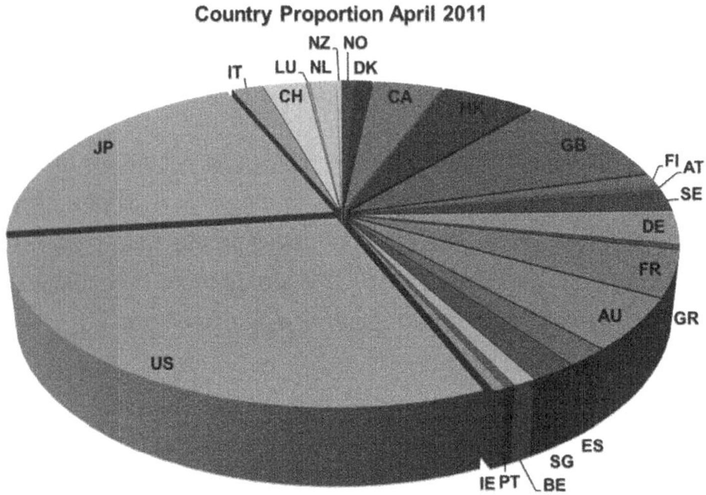


Figure 7: Global Market - country proportions (April 2011)

context it is important to point out the countries affiliated in the STOXX Global 1800 index to tackle the objective how the recent crisis affected Japan. Table 3 provides the changes within the index and a list of the country abbreviations which are drawn to throughout this dissertation.

Table 3: Changes in country allocations

| | Code | Country | Nov 2010 | Apr 2011 | Index Weight in % | Changes in total |
|---|---|---|---|---|---|---|
| 1 | US | United States of America | 534 | 527 | 29,28% | -7 |
| 2 | JP | Japan | 377 | 370 | 20,56% | -7 |
| 3 | GB | Great Britain | 175 | 171 | 9,50% | -4 |
| 4 | HK | Hongkong | 86 | 98 | 5,44% | 12 |
| 5 | AU | Australia | 97 | 93 | 5,17% | -4 |
| 6 | FR | France | 83 | 83 | 4,61% | 0 |
| 7 | CA | Canada | 66 | 73 | 4,06% | 7 |
| 8 | DE | Germany | 58 | 60 | 3,33% | 2 |
| 9 | CH | Switzerland | 46 | 46 | 2,56% | 0 |
| 10 | SE | Sweden | 37 | 38 | 2,11% | 1 |
| 11 | SG | Singapore | 35 | 35 | 1,94% | 0 |
| 12 | ES | Spain | 33 | 32 | 1,78% | -1 |
| 13 | IT | Italy | 31 | 32 | 1,78% | 1 |
| 14 | NL | The Netherland | 28 | 29 | 1,61% | 1 |
| 15 | FI | Finland | 21 | 21 | 1,17% | 0 |
| 16 | DK | Denmark | 16 | 18 | 1,00% | 2 |
| 17 | BE | Belgium | 17 | 17 | 0,94% | 0 |
| 18 | NO | Norway | 15 | 15 | 0,83% | 0 |
| 19 | AT | Austria | 11 | 10 | 0,56% | -1 |
| 20 | IE | Ireland | 9 | 9 | 0,50% | 0 |
| 21 | GR | Greece | 9 | 8 | 0,44% | -1 |
| 22 | PT | Portugal | 9 | 8 | 0,44% | -1 |
| 23 | NZ | New Zealand | 5 | 4 | 0,22% | -1 |
| 24 | LU | Luxembourg | 2 | 3 | 0,17% | 1 |
| Total | | | 1800 | 1800 | 100,00% | 0 |

Similar to the findings of Odien & Solnik (1993), the USA play a major role in the World Market as they still count for nearly 70% of the market capitalisation. Table 3 shows that the situation has not changed dramatically over the last 18 years. In April 2011 the US stocks account for 29.3% of the index which strengthens the arguments above, demands for a global diversification, and invalidates the studies focussing on single countries to prove the hypotheses underlying the CAPM or the MPT theories.

A second important outcome of these figures are the changes especially in the North American (STOXX Americas 600) and the Eastern regions (STOXX Asia/Pacific 600). While the loss of the US stocks is due to the aftermath of the financial crisis followed by a reorientation towards the supersectors dominated by Canadian companies, the changes in the Asia/Pacific region show another derivation. First, the loss of Australia derives from the strong position of the Hong Kong market which proves the strength of the Chinese industry and their open market policy. Also for the benefit of this rising star 7 Japanese stocks lost their listing within the indices due to the recent crisis while Hong Kong established itself as the leading exchange for IPO's in the world in regards of raised capital according to a study of Ernst & Young (2011). Other causes for these dramatic changes could only be located by having a closer look on the supersectors (Figure 8).

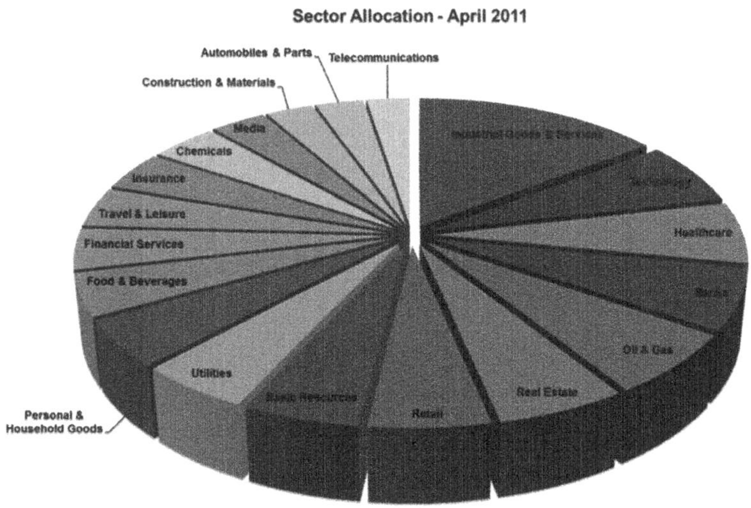


Figure 8: Global Market - Sector Allocation

"Industrial Goods & Services" is by far the biggest supersector and accounts for 14.89% of the World Market. The runner-ups are "Technology, Banks, Healthcare and Oil & Gas" with around 6.5%. The least important ones are "Construction & Materials, Automobiles & Parts and Telecommunications" at less than 3%. In the six months testing period there have been remarkable changes within the supersectors, deriving from the financial crisis and disasters in Japan. The rising of some supersectors can be attributed to improved economic surroundings which regularly show positive influences on cyclical sectors like "Automobiles, Chemicals" and other durables. This accompanies the findings of an Allianz Global Investors (2009) study which analysed 10 sectors using a data sample provided by Datastream in the period 1973-2008. According to their study those sectors perform better than neutral or defensive sectors when global markets experience growth phases, an economic pick-up or a boom. The findings of this work show similar results as it is shown in table 4.

Table 4: Changes in supersector allocations

| | Supersector | Nov 2010 | Apr 2011 | Index Weight in % | Changes in total | Changes in % |
|---|---|---|---|---|---|---|
| 1 | Industrial Goods & Services | 273 | 268 | 14,89% | -5 | -1,83% |
| 2 | Technology | 117 | 119 | 6,61% | 2 | 1,71% |
| 3 | Healthcare | 120 | 116 | 6,44% | -4 | -3,33% |
| 4 | Banks | 129 | 116 | 6,44% | -13 | -10,08% |
| 5 | Oil & Gas | 114 | 116 | 6,44% | 2 | 1,75% |
| 6 | Real Estate | 93 | 104 | 5,78% | 11 | 11,83% |
| 7 | Retail | 98 | 96 | 5,33% | -2 | -2,04% |
| 8 | Basic Resources | 92 | 93 | 5,17% | 1 | 1,09% |
| 9 | Utilities | 92 | 90 | 5,00% | -2 | -2,17% |
| 10 | Personal & Household Goods | 88 | 88 | 4,89% | 0 | 0,00% |
| 11 | Food & Beverages | 80 | 81 | 4,50% | 1 | 1,25% |
| 12 | Financial Services | 76 | 77 | 4,28% | 1 | 1,32% |
| 13 | Travel & Leisure | 75 | 75 | 4,17% | 0 | 0,00% |
| 14 | Insurance | 78 | 75 | 4,17% | -3 | -3,85% |
| 15 | Chemicals | 71 | 74 | 4,11% | 3 | 4,23% |
| 16 | Media | 54 | 61 | 3,39% | 7 | 12,96% |
| 17 | Construction & Materials | 58 | 52 | 2,89% | -6 | -10,34% |
| 18 | Automobiles & Parts | 47 | 52 | 2,89% | 5 | 10,64% |
| 19 | Tele-communications | 45 | 47 | 2,61% | 2 | 4,44% |
| Total | | 1800 | 1800 | 100,00% | 0 | |

Furthermore, the researchers (Allianz Global Investors 2009) argued that in most cases cyclicality and the beta of sectors run parallel. That this is true for six out of ten sectors immediately shows the drawback of this conclusion. Having a closer look at the findings one sees the correlation between beta risk and cyclicality for small beta sectors which all are defensive sectors at the same time (three out of three). Within the study conducted and the findings given in table 4 it can be argued that the cyclical sectors outperformed the others because the allocation of the index depends on the market capitalisation which rises if at least one of its two constituent parts shows an increase: the number of shares (through IPOs and SPOs) or the stock price. Some of the changes can be explained by IPOs, but besides three big transactions in Hong Kong and one in the U.S. in 2010 (Ernst & Young 2011) the IPO market was weak in the last year and is now slowly beginning to revive. Most of the changes are caused by increased stock prices of the existing free float (publicly tradable) of outstanding shares. The next section will give detailed information about the stock betas and returns for the whole market proxy and afterwards for each of the sectors.

## 4.4 Beta and Return Analysis

### *4.4.1 Descriptive Statistics*

#### *4.4.1.1 World Market*

First of all this section informs about beta risk and return for the complete World Market by conducting an univariate analysis. To give an overview table 5 demonstrates the most important measures of central tendency and dispersion for both investigated periods.

Table 5: Univariate Analysis of the World Market

| | Average | Mean | Standard deviation |
|---|---|---|---|
| **Nov 10** | | | |
| beta | 1,04 | 0,94 | 0,68 |
| return | 21,55% | 18,47% | 0,31 |
| **Apr 11** | | | |
| beta | 0,94 | 0,92 | 0,60 |
| return | 10,00% | 7,98% | 0,28 |

It is apparent that beta risk is quite stable over time which is absolutely consistent with theory. In reflection of the literature review it has to be mentioned that the aggregated betas of all securities should sum up to 1 as implicated by the CAPM. This is not the case in both periods. This could derive from the already mentioned drawback of this proxy. Even though this is one of the biggest samples investigated, it must be recognised that only the biggest, most liquid 1,800 companies are listed in this index. In respect to the theory, smaller and less liquid stocks are distinguished as conspicuously riskier than the aforementioned blue chips. If these stocks would be added to the proxy used in this dissertation, the market beta would reach the expected beta of 1. Subsequently, a closer look at the sectors explains how supersectors vary regarding betas and returns compared to each other and over the time periods.

#### *4.4.1.2 Supersectors*

The subsequent tables present a major outcome of this work. It shows that differences between the 19 supersectors exist considering beta and return.

Table 6: Descriptive Supersector Analysis - April 2011

| Supersector | Return | | | Beta | | |
|---|---|---|---|---|---|---|
| | Average | Mean | Standard deviation | Average | Mean | Standard deviation |
| Automobiles & Parts | 23,92% | 13,00% | 40,89% | 1,13 | 1,18 | 0,45 |
| Banks | -9,83% | -10,38% | 19,22% | 1,04 | 1,00 | 0,48 |
| Basic Resources | 16,19% | 10,39% | 45,91% | 1,56 | 1,56 | 0,55 |
| Chemicals | 22,17% | 20,12% | 26,08% | 0,94 | 0,85 | 0,37 |
| Construction & Materials | 6,54% | 7,94% | 20,39% | 1,07 | 1,21 | 0,44 |
| Financial Services | 12,08% | 9,38% | 26,18% | 1,12 | 1,11 | 0,36 |
| Food & Beverages | 9,73% | 7,43% | 23,92% | 0,58 | 0,52 | 0,33 |
| Healthcare | 9,59% | 6,77% | 25,33% | 0,59 | 0,54 | 0,50 |
| Industrial Goods & Services | 13,09% | 11,54% | 23,52% | 1,04 | 1,00 | 0,39 |
| Insurance | 8,04% | 6,76% | 17,30% | 1,04 | 0,91 | 0,51 |
| Media | 7,25% | 6,01% | 20,56% | 0,94 | 0,89 | 0,51 |
| Oil & Gas | 18,67% | 16,65% | 23,42% | 1,22 | 1,19 | 0,66 |
| Personal & Household Goods | 7,72% | 2,87% | 31,71% | 0,79 | 0,79 | 0,46 |
| Real Estate | 12,37% | 13,26% | 18,77% | 0,96 | 0,99 | 0,51 |
| Retail | 3,90% | 4,53% | 23,63% | 0,72 | 0,72 | 0,45 |
| Technology | 5,12% | 3,40% | 31,57% | 0,89 | 0,97 | 1,21 |
| Telecommunications | 13,88% | 12,04% | 20,13% | 0,65 | 0,60 | 0,37 |
| Travel & Leisure | 9,81% | 1,29% | 39,97% | 0,89 | 0,91 | 0,58 |
| Utilities | 5,82% | 4,62% | 26,92% | 0,54 | 0,53 | 0,36 |

A closer look at two supersectors with an aggregated beta mean reaching 1.00 gives an extreme example that there is no perfect relation between beta and return. While "Industrial Goods & Services" increased during the period 4/2010-4/2011 by 11.54%, "Banks" decreased by 10.38%. An also very interesting finding is given by "Chemicals" which reached the highest return (20.12%) although the supersector is less risky as the market in total (beta: 0.85). These results are illustrated by figure 9 where returns are connected with the betas of the supersectors. Afterwards the findings are compared with those provided by the observation conducted in November 2010. It becomes obvious that sectors like "Real Estate", "Industrial Goods & Services" and also "Healthcare" and "Utilities" show a balanced risk-return relation and therefore should be equal-weighted in a portfolio to be effective. Others, like "Basic Resources", "Banks" or "Construction & Materials", should be underweighted while "Chemicals" & "Telecommunications" should be overweighted if wanting to outperform the Global Market without being confronted with a higher systematic risk. To validate this finding table 7 provides a retrospect on the examination conducted in November 2010.

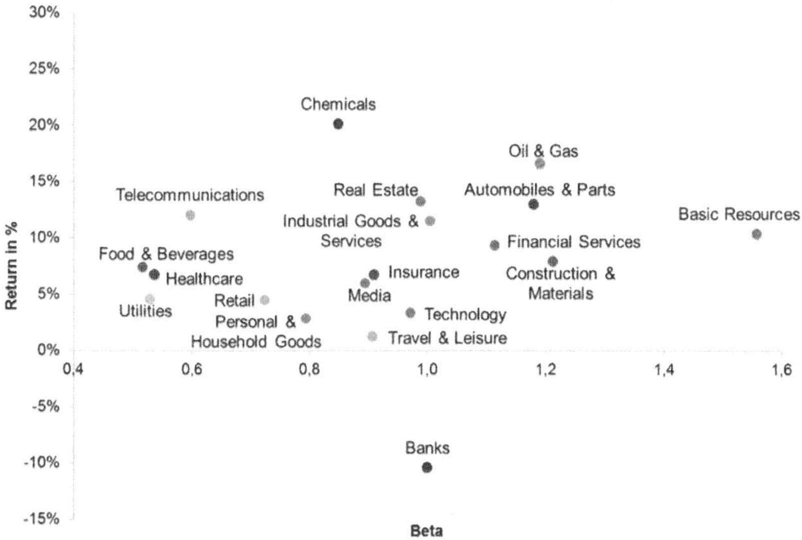


Figure 9: Beta vs. Return - Supersectors (April 2011)

Similar to the findings of April 2011 "Industrial Goods & Services" and "Technology" showed major difference in returns of 14.06%. Very remarkable is that supersectors with the highest return differ dramatically regarding their beta. Both of them gained a return of over 30% while "Industrial Goods & Services" owns a beta of 0.99, "Basic Resources" has one of 1.56, the highest of all sectors. One can conclude that there is a linear relation between those parameters. However, as discussed before, it is a false friend.

Table 7: Descriptive Supersector Analysis - November 2010

| Supersector | Return | | | Beta | | |
|---|---|---|---|---|---|---|
| | Average | Mean | Standard deviation | Average | Mean | Standard deviation |
| Automobiles & Parts | 27,45% | 26,30% | 34% | 1,02 | 0,90 | 0,61 |
| Banks | 1,00% | -4,07% | 27% | 1,26 | 1,19 | 0,70 |
| Basic Resources | 30,06% | 22,81% | 39% | 1,56 | 1,56 | 0,65 |
| Chemicals | 28,37% | 26,48% | 28% | 0,99 | 0,90 | 0,44 |
| Construction & Materials | 4,64% | 2,98% | 24% | 1,09 | 1,15 | 0,47 |
| Financial Services | 16,06% | 14,22% | 24% | 1,34 | 1,23 | 0,54 |
| Food & Beverages | 28,51% | 25,95% | 24% | 0,76 | 0,71 | 1,05 |
| Healthcare | 19,92% | 15,15% | 27% | 0,67 | 0,64 | 0,50 |
| Industrial Goods & Services | 30,90% | 28,33% | 30% | 1,06 | 0,99 | 0,51 |
| Insurance | 8,75% | 9,59% | 18% | 1,32 | 1,11 | 0,81 |
| Media | 26,51% | 26,69% | 20% | 0,96 | 0,88 | 0,54 |
| Oil & Gas | 11,45% | 7,29% | 30% | 1,51 | 1,53 | 0,56 |
| Personal & Household Goods | 26,13% | 23,71% | 30% | 0,79 | 0,71 | 0,48 |
| Real Estate | 29,38% | 22,91% | 24% | 1,11 | 1,06 | 0,65 |
| Retail | 25,41% | 17,41% | 36% | 0,81 | 0,75 | 0,65 |
| Technology | 21,40% | 14,27% | 34% | 0,97 | 1,00 | 0,77 |
| Telecommunications | 26,08% | 24,69% | 26% | 0,84 | 0,75 | 0,59 |
| Travel & Leisure | 26,07% | 21,71% | 35% | 0,88 | 0,90 | 0,78 |
| Utilities | 15,16% | 16,30% | 23% | 0,58 | 0,62 | 0,47 |

In order to analyse supersectors which are generally more risky and predicted to gain higher profits, the next table provides a deviation analysis. Table 8 shows that betas normally do not fluctuate very intensively as 11 out of the 19 supersectors show less than a two-digit difference in "Basic Resources, Media, Travel & Leisure and Industrial Goods & Services".

Table 8: Changes in Supersector Betas

| Changes in Beta Risk | | | | | |
|---|---|---|---|---|---|
| Automobiles & Parts | Banks | Basic Resources | Chemicals | Construction & Materials | Financial Services |
| 0,28 | -0,19 | 0,00 | -0,05 | 0,06 | -0,12 |
| Food & Beverages | Healthcare | Industrial Goods & Services | Insurance | Media | Oil & Gas |
| -0,19 | -0,10 | 0,01 | -0,20 | 0,01 | -0,34 |
| Personal & Household Goods | Real Estate | Retail | Technology | Telecommunications | Travel & Leisure |
| 0,08 | -0,07 | -0,03 | -0,03 | -0,15 | 0,01 |
| Utilities | | | | | |
| -0,09 | | | | | |

Others seem to be, positively or negatively, heavily affected by economic changes like "Oil & Gas" (beta decrease: 0.34) or Automobile & Parts (beta increase: 0.28). The findings above are very important for the creation of a portfolio allocation based on the MPT and the CAPM which is illustrated by figure 10, again showing the relationship between beta risk and return.

Figure 10: Beta vs. Return - Supersectors (November 2010)

In November 2010 it is patently obvious that investments in "Telecommunications" and Food & Beverages" were superefficient towards those in "Oil & Gas" or Construction & Materials" from the viewpoint of an investor who was risk averse and a return optimiser. While betas are quite constant over time the returns of supersectors are highly influenced by economic incidents and natural disasters as we can see by the example of "Oil & Gas". This sector suffered extremely from the oil spill in the Gulf of Mexico in May 2010 which ensued in an increase in beta and a decrease in returns.

Therefore, it is unrewarding to allocate uncorrelated stocks from a single supersector even if the latter has the same beta as the market itself. In the next section a closer look on the country specifics, in particular those of Japan, are given to complete the descriptive analysis of the World Market and to gain further knowledge about external impacts.

#### *4.4.1.3 Regional Markets and Single Countries*

In order to gain further knowledge on the risk-return relationship within and across countries it is important to know if a country's economy is strongly connected to single supersectors, as shown in table 9. In this case only the data for April 2011 is examined as the comparative advantage of a country does not change over time according to Krugman & Obstfeld (2008). A remarkable finding of this observation is that some countries possess a well-diversified economy (highlighted in green) while others are heavily dependent on single sectors. Even though Hong Kong and Canada have more listed companies in the STOXX Global 1800 index as for example Germany, their economy is poorly diversified. The biggest sector of those two countries accounts for a fourth of the total listings. A negatively event within such an important sector could go beyond a national economic crisis. This situation worsens if a country's economy is comparatively small. In Greece for example, where the banking sector allocates 50% of all listed companies, this sector was extremely affected by the financial crisis, before the total Greek economy was sucked into this whirlpool, and then it lately splashed over whole Europe. In addition, such a concentration on single supersectors does involve that especially the Greek market cannot be seen as efficient according to the EMH. This argumentation is supported by the recent studies of Cajueiro *et al.* (2009) and Dicle & Levendis (2011). As the basic assumption, the existence of an efficient market, is missing, a verification of the CAPM as the right model to explain the cross-section of stock returns leads to false results.

Table 9: Country dependency on Supersectors

| Country | Biggest Sector | Proportion in % | Runner-Up | Proportion in % (biggest + runner-up) |
|---|---|---|---|---|
| Australia | Basic Resources | 17% | Real Estate | 29% |
| Austria | Banks | 20% | Construction & Materials | 30% |
| Belgium | Financial Services | 24% | Banks | 35% |
| Canada | Oil & Gas | 27% | Basic Resources | 45% |
| Denmark | Healthcare | 28% | Banks | 44% |
| Finland | Industrial Goods & Services | 24% | Basic Resources | 43% |
| France | Industrial Goods & Services | 17% | Media | 28% |
| Germany | Industrial Goods & Services | 15% | Chemicals | 28% |
| Great Britain | Industrial Goods & Services | 19% | Financial Services | 27% |
| Greece | Banks | 50% | Telecommunications | 63% |
| Hong Kong | Real Estate | 23% | Industrial Goods & Services | 36% |
| Ireland | Travel & Leisure | 22% | Food & Beverages | 44% |
| Italy | Banks | 31% | Utilities | 47% |
| Japan | Industrial Goods & Services | 19% | Chemicals | 27% |
| Luxembourg | Basic Resources | 67% | Media | 100% |
| New Zealand | Telecommunication | 25% | Utilities | 50% |
| Netherlands | Food & Beverages | 17% | Industrial Goods & Services | 34% |
| Norway | Oil & Gas | 47% | Food & Beverages | 60% |
| Portugal | Banks | 25% | Utilities | 50% |
| Singapore | Real Estate | 26% | Industrial Goods & Services | 46% |
| Spain | Banks | 19% | Utilities | 38% |
| Sweden | Industrial Goods & Services | 24% | Personal & Household Goods | 37% |
| Switzerland | Healthcare | 17% | Industrial Goods & Services | 33% |
| USA | Industrial Goods & Services | 13% | Technology | 25% |

Another important reason to diversify across multiple countries can also be derived from table 9. The best diversification across supersectors can be adjudicated to the USA which at first glance might alleviate the criticism passed on academics and researchers who used a proxy of the US stock market to synthesize the Global stock market. However, even in a globalised, industrialised and foremost peaceful world there are incidents which can extremely affect single countries and their economies. Japan, to pick up a recent example, is quite as well-diversified as the USA but was hit by crisis which almost exclusively influenced its own economy. As a portfolio allocated of stocks of a single country is exposed to the systematic risk of this country, only an international index would provide a reasonable diversification for a valid proxy.

Table 10 again uses descriptive statistics to nail down the argumentation stated above. It is important to have a look at both periods to explain that incidents might affect single countries. The focus especially lays on Japan and Greece to follow up on the above mentioned examples.

Table 10: Descriptive Country Analysis - April 2011

| Country | Return | | | Beta | | |
|---|---|---|---|---|---|---|
| | Average | Mean | Standard deviation | Average | Mean | Standard deviation |
| Australia | 14,14% | 9,55% | 0,43 | 1,40 | 1,33 | 0,76 |
| Austria | 13,57% | 9,17% | 0,16 | 1,16 | 1,19 | 0,47 |
| Belgium | 21,01% | 17,67% | 0,30 | 0,91 | 0,76 | 0,53 |
| Canada | 16,75% | 12,02% | 0,28 | 1,04 | 1,12 | 0,50 |
| Denmark | 14,72% | 10,33% | 0,27 | 0,76 | 0,88 | 0,38 |
| Finland | 27,21% | 30,11% | 0,26 | 1,08 | 1,08 | 0,35 |
| France | 18,23% | 13,24% | 0,24 | 1,12 | 1,07 | 0,41 |
| Germany | 23,66% | 23,25% | 0,25 | 1,07 | 1,10 | 0,38 |
| Great Britain | 16,64% | 15,12% | 0,27 | 1,05 | 1,01 | 0,48 |
| Greece | -23,18% | -19,96% | 0,24 | 0,78 | 0,78 | 0,29 |
| Hong Kong | 12,53% | 5,59% | 0,46 | 0,78 | 0,87 | 1,32 |
| Ireland | -1,38% | 6,40% | 0,29 | 1,00 | 0,87 | 0,75 |
| Italy | 9,55% | 9,20% | 0,29 | 0,90 | 0,95 | 0,43 |
| Japan | -4,75% | -6,08% | 0,22 | 0,56 | 0,55 | 0,40 |
| Luxembourg | -1,80% | -1,80% | 0,09 | 0,88 | 0,50 | 0,65 |
| Netherlands | 10,96% | 12,10% | 0,16 | 1,01 | 0,97 | 0,44 |
| New Zealand | 13,91% | 16,80% | 0,13 | 0,73 | 0,76 | 0,41 |
| Norway | 19,78% | 21,47% | 0,14 | 1,57 | 1,57 | 0,31 |
| Portugal | 8,07% | 3,27% | 0,24 | 0,70 | 0,79 | 0,18 |
| Singapore | 17,72% | 12,62% | 0,24 | 0,76 | 0,71 | 0,42 |
| Spain | 12,42% | 13,04% | 0,22 | 0,75 | 0,68 | 0,32 |
| Sweden | 30,00% | 27,55% | 0,26 | 1,20 | 1,22 | 0,30 |
| Switzerland | 23,10% | 28,22% | 0,23 | 0,88 | 0,83 | 0,40 |
| USA | 9,19% | 7,53% | 0,22 | 1,06 | 0,99 | 0,49 |

Unsurprisingly the results of the descriptive analysis of countries incorporated in the STOXX Global 1800 index are similar to those of the supersector analysis. Taking a look at two countries which aggregated beta means reaching approximately 1.00 gives an example that there is no perfect relation between beta and return, but the difference between their return is considerably smaller. While US-stocks went up 7.53% the British securities increased 15.12% in the period 4/2010-4/2011 which still is an outperformance of over a 100%. On the other hand two countries with almost similar returns like Germany (23.25%) and Norway (21.47%) clearly differ in their beta risk (Germany: 1.10 vs. Norway: 1.57). Similar to the supersector example of "Chemicals", Switzerland, a country with one of the lowest beta values (0.88) reached one of the highest returns (28.22%). Connected to the findings about the supersectors combined with the comparative advantage some countries have in special sectors, the amplitude of the return variations might raise. This can be positive like in Switzerland where the biggest sectors (Healthcare, Industrial Goods & Services) gain high returns on comparatively low betas or negative, like in Australia where only average profits can be made from risky investments in their biggest sectors (Basic Resources, Real Estate). Figure 11 illustrates the usefulness to choose a country diversification due to the big differences in the beta-return relation.

Figure 11: Beta vs. Return - Countries (April 2011)

Here, it becomes obvious that investments in countries like Great Britain, France and the Netherlands should be equal-weighted to create a portfolio seeking to be risk-return efficient. If investments in countries like Switzerland or Finland are overweighted while they are underweight in Norway or Greece, a portfolio could outperform the Global Market.

To testify these findings table 11 looks back on the ones examined in November 2010. In general, the beta means across all countries reached a higher level in November 2010 than six months later (-0.16). The same can be realised by having a look on the returns across all sectors which shows the uncertainty of investors or a higher inherent systematic risk. It can be concluded that this decrease in risk is followed by lower returns and therefore the CAPM holds true in regards to a linear beta-risk relation. This is quite different to the results of the supersector analysis where the mean of all sector betas was stable over time (approx.: 0.90) and the returns decreased from November 2010 (21.71%) to April 2011 (7.43%).

Table 11: Descriptive Country Analysis - November 2010

| Country | Return | | | Beta | | |
|---|---|---|---|---|---|---|
| | Average | Mean | Standard deviation | Average | Mean | Standard deviation |
| Australia | 24,99% | 21,02% | 0,30 | 1,24 | 1,17 | 0,58 |
| Austria | 3,42% | -1,32% | 0,20 | 1,12 | 1,14 | 0,59 |
| Belgium | 19,52% | 8,56% | 0,35 | 0,95 | 0,81 | 0,68 |
| Canada | 30,75% | 24,62% | 0,41 | 1,23 | 1,23 | 0,60 |
| Denmark | 24,02% | 30,24% | 0,31 | 1,62 | 1,14 | 2,07 |
| Finland | 34,88% | 34,52% | 0,28 | 1,14 | 1,21 | 0,35 |
| France | 15,44% | 9,87% | 0,26 | 1,16 | 1,14 | 0,57 |
| Germany | 17,68% | 18,38% | 0,24 | 1,24 | 1,16 | 0,43 |
| Great Britain | 29,37% | 26,50% | 0,31 | 1,14 | 1,06 | 0,57 |
| Greece | -40,99% | -54,30% | 0,28 | 1,00 | 1,10 | 0,53 |
| Hong Kong | 33,59% | 31,16% | 0,28 | 0,70 | 0,77 | 0,83 |
| Ireland | 2,97% | 13,50% | 0,32 | 1,10 | 0,83 | 0,93 |
| Italy | -2,52% | -7,55% | 0,23 | 1,01 | 0,98 | 0,40 |
| Japan | 8,31% | 6,40% | 0,22 | 0,49 | 0,52 | 0,40 |
| Luxembourg | 7,38% | 7,38% | 0,11 | 1,27 | 1,27 | 1,03 |
| Netherlands | 20,01% | 19,68% | 0,24 | 1,06 | 0,92 | 0,53 |
| New Zealand | 2,55% | -5,60% | 0,28 | 0,75 | 0,90 | 0,27 |
| Norway | 27,52% | 31,71% | 0,27 | 1,73 | 1,86 | 0,44 |
| Portugal | -4,23% | -11,42% | 0,33 | 0,81 | 0,81 | 0,24 |
| Singapore | 49,31% | 46,71% | 0,26 | 0,88 | 0,91 | 0,41 |
| Spain | -7,17% | -9,13% | 0,24 | 0,92 | 0,84 | 0,34 |
| Sweden | 48,16% | 42,53% | 0,27 | 1,31 | 1,27 | 0,32 |
| Switzerland | 23,74% | 20,90% | 0,31 | 0,98 | 0,97 | 0,51 |
| USA | 27,02% | 24,89% | 0,30 | 1,32 | 1,21 | 0,66 |

An overall view is given in table 12. It shows that the betas of most of the analysed countries did not change significantly, so by less than 0.1 (12 out of 24).

Table 12: Changes in Country betas

| | | | | | |
|---|---|---|---|---|---|
| Australia | Austria | Belgium | Canada | Denmark | Finland |
| 0,16 | 0,05 | -0,06 | -0,11 | -0,26 | -0,13 |
| France | Germany | Great Britain | Greece | Hong Kong | Ireland |
| -0,07 | -0,06 | -0,06 | -0,32 | 0,09 | 0,04 |
| Italy | Japan | Luxembourg | Netherlands | New Zealand | Norway |
| -0,03 | 0,03 | -0,77 | 0,06 | -0,14 | -0,28 |
| Portugal | Singapore | Spain | Sweden | Switzerland | USA |
| -0,02 | -0,20 | -0,16 | -0,05 | -0,14 | -0,22 |

Exceptions are constituted by countries which proportion in the index changed significantly like Luxembourg and by countries which are extremely dependent on single supersectors like Greece or Norway. To better illustrate the data figure 12 shows the differences regarding risk-return relation of the countries in November 2010. The statements given above still hold true regarding the creation of an efficient portfolio, even though there are indications that some anomalies were apparent in November 2010 where Hong Kong and Singapore impressed with very high returns at quite low betas. In other words the question might be raised if those markets can be regarded as efficient in accordance to the EMH.

Figure 12: Beta vs. Return - Countries (November 2010)

Furthermore, the results for Japan are quite interesting, while the betas of Japanese Stocks related to the Global Market did not change dramatically, the returns decreased significantly. It becomes obvious that the recent incidents in this country are unsystematic from a global viewpoint and diversifiable. Not surprisingly, the decrease in return derived from those supersectors which were most affected by the catastrophes: Utilities (-17.40%), Travel & Leisure (-12.48%), Technology (-19.78%), and the Financial sectors.

### *4.4.1.4 Summary*

Figures 13 & 14 illustrate which sectors are beta-return efficient and which are not. The illustration summarises the findings from above. Therefore, a ratio is calculated by dividing the beta by the corresponding returns. The favourable sectors and countries are those which show the lowest positive value.

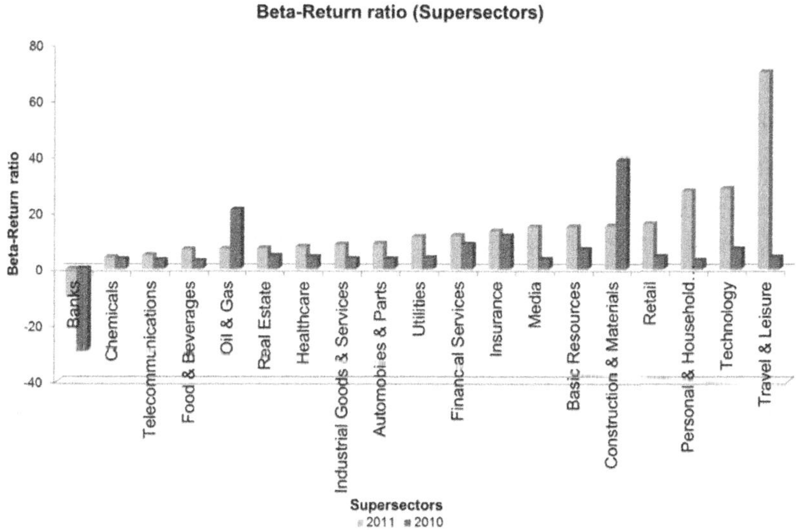


Figure 13: The Beta-Return ratio (Supersectors)

It can be stated that some sectors show a quite efficient risk-return relation like "Telecommunications", "Chemicals" and "Food & Beverages" which are steadily able to outperform the market while others like the three sectors of the financial industry and "Construction & Materials" are steadily risk-return inefficient.

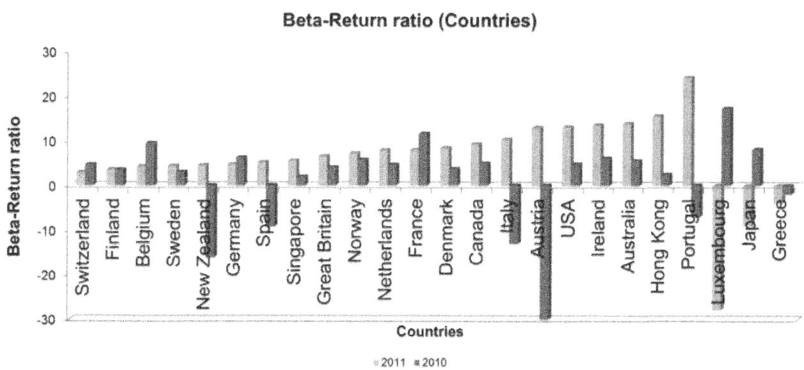


Figure 14: Beta-Return ratio (Countries)

It becomes obvious that some countries are risk-return efficient over time, for example Switzerland and Finland. Other markets like New Zealand, Luxembourg and Austria are not stable in the long run as these markets cannot be regarded as efficient in the sense of the EMH. Japan constitutes an exception due to the effects of the recent natural disasters. The impacts of the Euro crisis negatively affected Greece, Portugal, Italy, and Spain which points out the economic problems.

In summary, an efficient portfolio should be constructed by a well-structured diversification over countries and supersectors as both of them show individual and interacting impacts in regards to the CAPM. How this can be approached is analysed and worked out in the subsequent section.

### *4.4.2 Building the model*

To meet the requirements of this work, stocks should be selected which allow the creation of a portfolio to be risk-return efficient and useful within a long-term investment strategy. Therefore, three portfolios of 95 stocks have been created, using different predictor variables: return, beta and a beta-return ratio. The latter one is calculated by simply dividing the beta by the return. Afterwards, the stocks are ranked where the favourable one are those which show the lowest positive ratios as they either have a comparatively high return (low betas) or an optimal combination thereof. This is done by using the data of November 2010. Hereafter, it is analysed how well these portfolios relate to the Global Market regarding the country and supersector diversification. Then it will be analysed how well the predictor variables forecasted the stock markets, so which stocks outperforming the market in November 2010 were still doing so in April 2011.

#### 4.4.2.1 "Return"-Portfolio

This portfolio consists of 95 stocks which gained the highest returns in the period 11/2009-11/2010 within the STOXX Global 1800 index. Table 13 illustrates the descriptive results of the comparison with the index itself. The table shows quite clearly the outperformance of the market which goes hand in hand with a distinctly higher beta and therefore, the CAPM seems to hold true. While the standard deviation is similar regarding the returns it shows that dispersion of returns is the same as in the total market. On the other hand the betas are not only higher, they vary much more strongly in the "Return"-portfolio.

Table 13: Return Portfolio vs. Global Market

| | Return | | | Beta | | |
|---|---|---|---|---|---|---|
| | **Average** | **Mean** | **Standard deviation** | **Average** | **Mean** | **Standard deviation** |
| **Best 95 - Return** | 99,07% | 87,84% | 30,57% | 1,28 | 1,29 | 0,99 |
| **STOXX Global 1800** | 21,55% | 18,47% | 30,56% | 1,04 | 0,94 | 0,68 |
| **Difference (Excess-)** | 77,52% | 69,37% | 0,01% | 0,25 | 0,35 | 0,30 |

Figures 15 & 16 illustrate how well this portfolio reflects the Global Market by considering the diversification across countries and sectors.

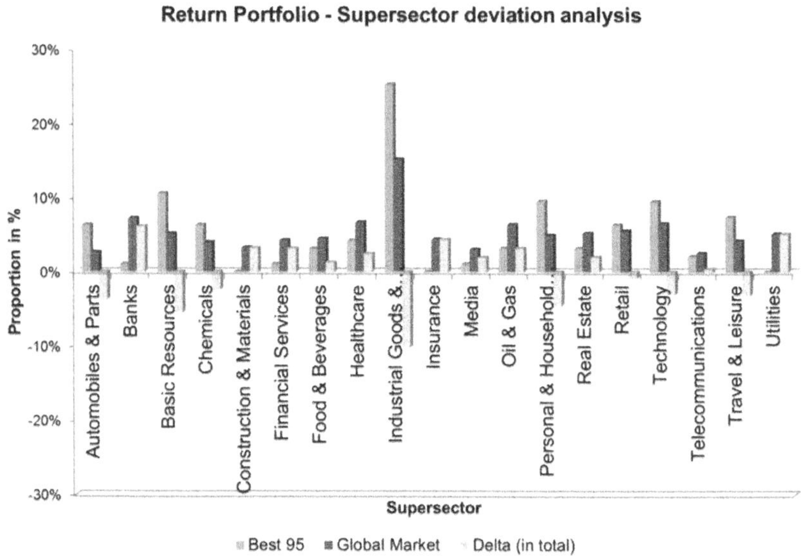


Figure 15: Deviation Analysis of Supersector Diversification – Return Portfolio

It is quite interesting that stocks of three supersectors ("Construction & Materials", "Insurance", "Utilities") are not under the 95 best performers, some are extremely overweighted ("Automobiles & Parts", "Personal & Household Goods", "Industrial Goods & Services"), most of them underweighted and only two are quite near to an equal-weight ("Telecommunications", "Retail"). Beside these findings, a short look on correlations show a strong positive linear dependency between the market proxy and the "Return"-portfolio for both sector (0.76) and country (0.83) allocations. This seems to be quite irritating as the diversification across countries of the "Return"-portfolio is strikingly different to the market allocation as stocks of 10 out of 24 countries were not placed under the 95 top performers as can be taken from the figure below. Only four countries (Australia, Belgium, Great Britain, and USA) could be regarded as equally-weighted while others (Japan and Germany) are strongly underweighted whereas Sweden and Singapore were overweighted.

In order to answer the question, if return is a good (valid) predictor variable to forecast stock market developments, it must be said that only 25 stocks out of 95 "Return"-portfolio examined in November 2010 are still under the top 95 in April 2011. These 25 reached a performance of 97.11% during the 11/2009-11/2010 period and 69.68% during the 4/2011-4/2011 period. The beta decreased from 1.57 (November 2010) to 1.39 (April 2011). Again, a linear dependency between beta and risk could be stated for this portfolio. The portfolio reached a mean risk-return ratio of 1.62 in November 2010 and 2.0 in April 2011.

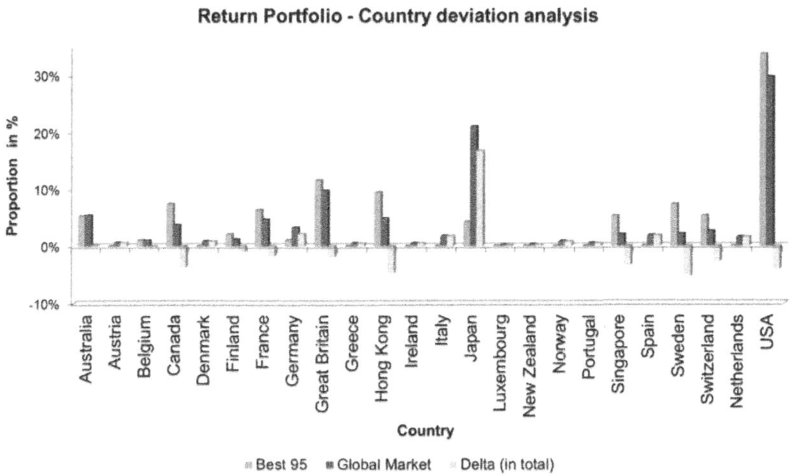


Figure 16: Deviation Analysis of Country Diversification

#### 4.4.2.2 *"Beta"-Portfolio*

This portfolio consists of 95 stocks which contain the lowest positive betas in the period 11/2009-11/2010 within the STOXX Global 1800 index. Table 14 illustrates the descriptive results of the comparison with the index itself.

Table 14: Beta Portfolio vs. Global Market

| | Return | | | Beta | | |
|---|---|---|---|---|---|---|
| | Average | Mean | Standard deviation | Average | Mean | Standard deviation |
| **Best 95 - Beta** | 14,50% | 11,48% | 27,55% | 0,18 | 0,18 | 0,08 |
| **STOXX Global 1800** | 21,55% | 18,47% | 30,56% | 1,04 | 0,94 | 0,68 |
| **Difference (Excess-)** | -7,04% | -6,99% | -3,01% | -0,86 | -0,76 | -0,60 |

It is quite evident that this portfolio almost wipes out the systematic risk as the beta decreases by 81%. Furthermore, the dispersion of the betas is reduced to a minimum. This kind of portfolio can be seen as the optimal choice for risk-averse investors. Again the CAPM seems to hold true as the reduction of beta goes along with a decrease of returns and thus this portfolio clearly underperformes the market. Figure 17 & 18 illustrate how well this portfolio reflects the Global Market by considering the diversification across countries and sectors.

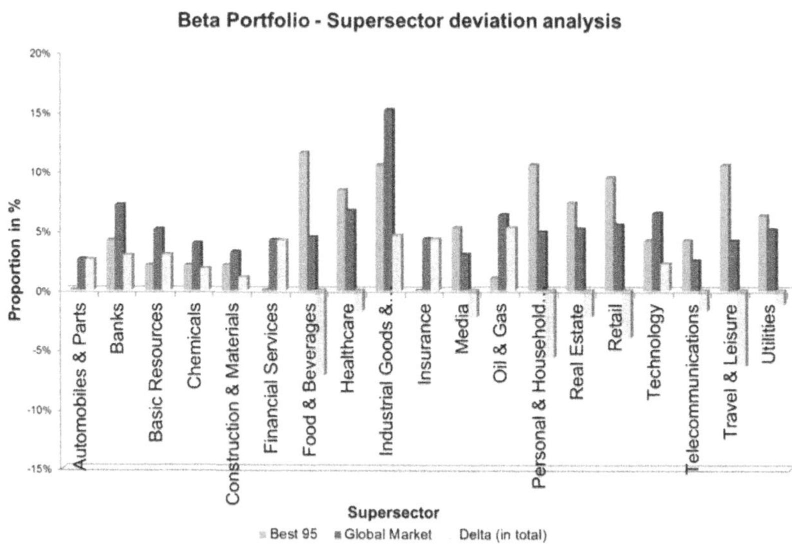


Figure 17: Deviation Analysis of Supersector Diversification – Beta Portfolio

Again, stocks of three supersectors ("Automobiles & Parts", "Financial Services", and "Insurance") are not under the 95 best performers. The most important and interesting perception here is that Insurance stocks are neither listed in the return portfolio nor in the beta portfolio. The sectors which are extremely overweighted are "Food & Beverages", "Personal & Household Goods", "Travel & Leisure". Here, one recognises that the sector "Food & Beverages" is overweighted in the "Beta"- and the "Return"-portfolio. Beside these findings, a short look on correlations show that the positive linear dependency between the market proxy and the "Beta"-portfolio is less strong for both sector (0.38) and country (0.58) allocations than it was the case within the "Return"-portfolio.

In the figure below it is illustrated that the "Beta"-portfolio is badly diversi fied across countries as stocks from eight countries are not allocated and only Canada and Italy are near to the weighting within the Global Market proxy. While all other countries are underweighted, most notably Great Britain and the USA, over 63% of this portfolio are allocated of Japanese stocks.

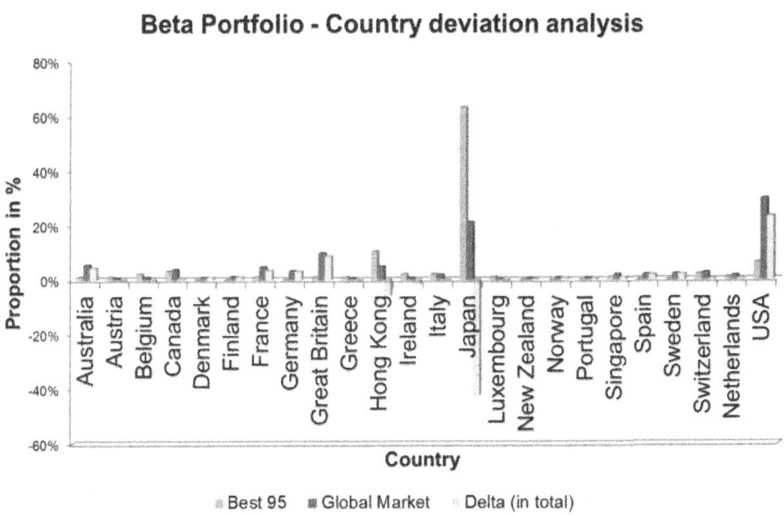


Figure 18: Deviation Analysis of Country Diversification – Beta Portfolio

To answer the question if beta is a good (valid) predictor variable, it can be said that 31 stocks out of 95 "Return"-portfolio examined in November 2010 are still in the top 95 in April 2011, so six more than "Return"-stocks. These 25 reached a performance of 7.36% during the 11/2009-11/2010 period and -2.82% during the 4/2011-4/2011 period. The beta remained almost stable (November 2010: 0.18; April 2011: 0.17). Again, a linear dependency between beta and risk can be stated for this portfolio. The portfolio reached a mean risk-return ratio of 2.48 in November 2010 and -6.18 in April 2011 due to the return decrease which can foremost be attributed to incidents in Japan. In general, these findings neither support nor reject the CAPM as the fluctuations in return are quite small compared to those of the "Return"-portfolio. Furthermore, historical beta can be seen as a better predictor than historical returns.

#### *4.4.2.3 "Ratio"-Portfolio*

This portfolio consists of 95 stocks which show the lowest positive beta-return rations in the period 11/2009-11/2010 within the STOXX Global 1800 index. Table 15 illustrates the descriptive results of the comparison with the index itself.

Table 15: Beta/Return Portfolio vs. Global Market

| | Return | | | Beta | | |
|---|---|---|---|---|---|---|
| | Average | Mean | Standard deviation | Average | Mean | Standard deviation |
| **Best 95 - Beta/Return** | 60,28% | 51,87% | 44,77% | 0,38 | 0,32 | 0,32 |
| **STOXX Global 1800** | 21,55% | 18,47% | 30,56% | 1,04 | 0,94 | 0,68 |
| **Difference (Excess-)** | 38,73% | 33,40% | 14,21% | -0,66 | -0,62 | -0,37 |

The analysis of the "Ratio"-portfolio delivers interesting results as it outperforms the market by 33.4% while it reduces the systematic risk in relation to the Global Market by over 60% at the same time. Due to the construction of this ratio a higher dispersion in returns has to be accepted by the investors whereas the betas vary on a quite low level.

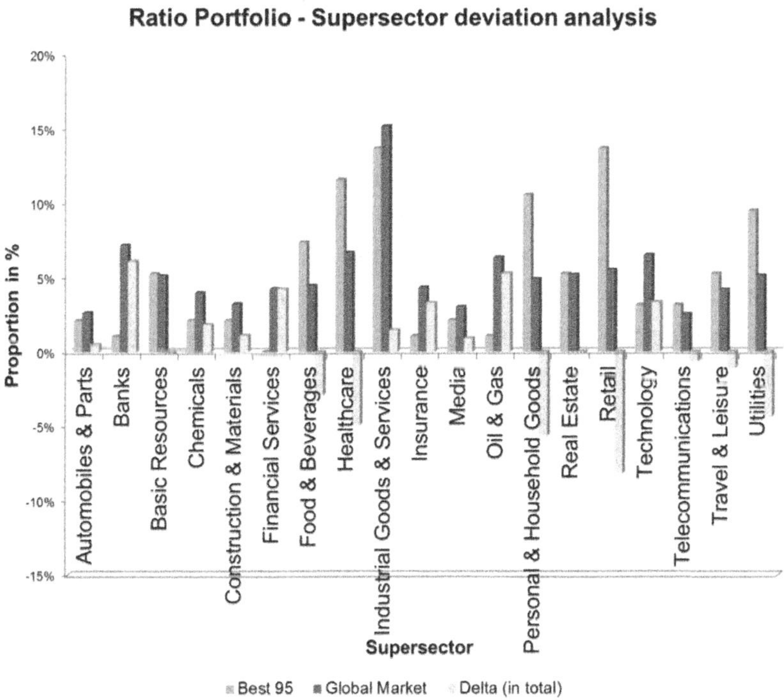


Figure 19: Deviation Analysis of Supersector Diversification – Ratio Portfolio

The interpretation of this data (Figure 19) shows two facts, firstly, the efficiency of the supersectors in regards to the risk-return relation and secondly, how well the diversification corresponds to that of the World Market. In contrast only the stocks of one supersector ("Financial Services") are not listed in the top 95 performers regarding the beta-return ratio. The other financial sectors ("Insurance", "Banks") follow shortly and even others like "Oil & Gas" are extremely underweighted in this portfolio. This shows that these supersectors cannot be regarded as risk-return efficient. Others show extremely high weights and can be regarded as very risk-return efficient; for example "Retail", "Personal & Household Goods", "Real Estate" and "Utilities". Taking a look at correlations, the leading risk-return efficient sectors are interdepend with the Global Market by 0.52 (sectors) and 0.86 (countries).

Figure 20 illustrates that only very few markets can be regarded as beta-return efficient. This depends strongly on the degree of market efficiency within the countries. A portfolio which seems to outperform the Global Market should first of all be effectively diversified over sectors. Due to the comparative advantages of countries in special sectors an efficient country allocation result as a logical consequence. It becomes obvious that some regional markets should be overweighted in such a risk-return portfolio like Great Britain, Hong Kong, Japan and Switzerland while the USA for example should be underweighted.

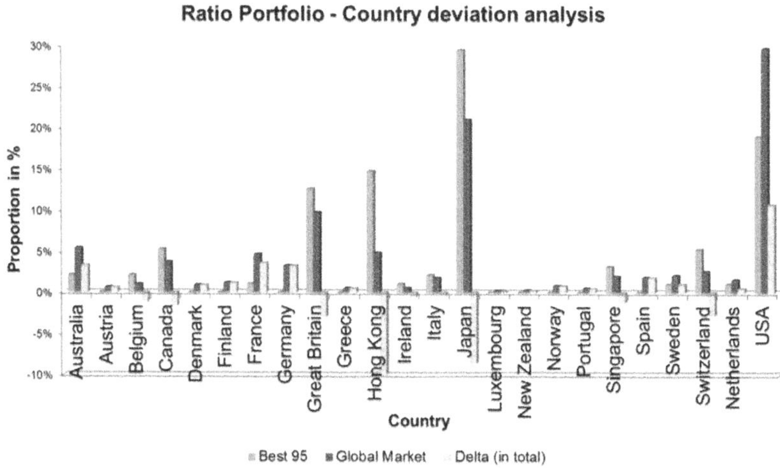


Figure 20: Deviation Analysis of Country Diversification – Ratio Portfolio

If the risk-return ratio is a useful (valid) predictor variable again the best performers were analysed. Only 25 stocks out of 95 "Ratio"-portfolio examined in November 2010 are still in the top 95 in April 2011. This is similar to the findings about the "return"-variable and less than those of the "beta"-variable. The 25 stocks with the lowest positive ratio reached a performance of 62.63% during the 11/2009-11/2010 period and

40.63% during the 4/2011-4/2011 period. The beta for this portfolio remained perfectly stable (November 2010: 0.32; April 2011: 0.32). Here, a linear dependency between beta and risk cannot be stated as the returns decreased over time but are still higher than those of the "beta"-portfolio. The portfolio reached a mean risk-return ratio of 0.52 in November 2010 and 0.8 in April 2011.

### 4.4.3 *Modelling of an efficient Portfolio allocation*

From an ex-post view proof has been found that it is possible to outperform the Global Market if stock-picking is undertaken by applying a supersector-oriented risk-return strategy. Figure 21 shows the most favourable sector allocation.

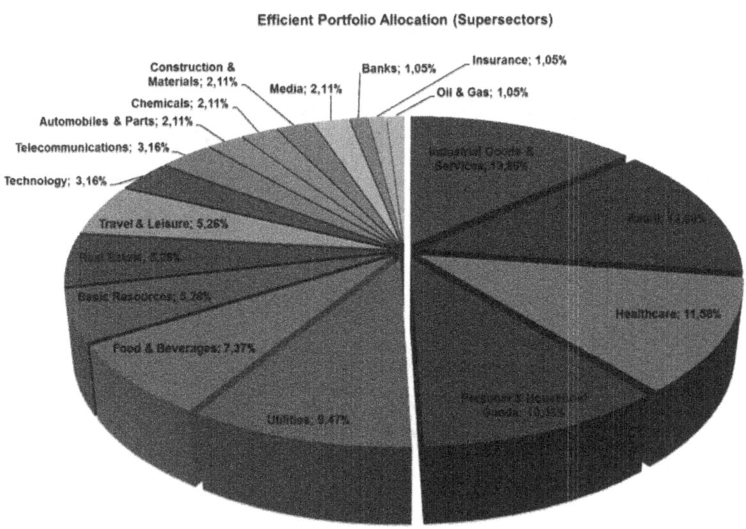


Figure 21: Efficient Supersector Allocation

As the country allocation of this portfolio is strongly dependent on the comparative advantages of countries the efficient portfolio shows the following country proportions (Figure 22). Unfortunately, it has not been possible so far to select single stocks which are steadily outperforming the Global Market. While the prediction is accuracy regarding comparatively low and stable betas, it is quite clear for single stocks that this is not the case regarding the expected returns. Here, other examinations have to be conducted which focuses on the behaviour of single stocks. Even though, the analysed data might be used as a valid foundation, it has to be enlarged by information like earnings announcements and longitudinal data which allows for statements about the question if and how stock returns are in general subject to long-time reversal effects, post earnings effects or momentum effects. Afterwards, it should be possible to sort the wheat from the chaff within the favourable sectors

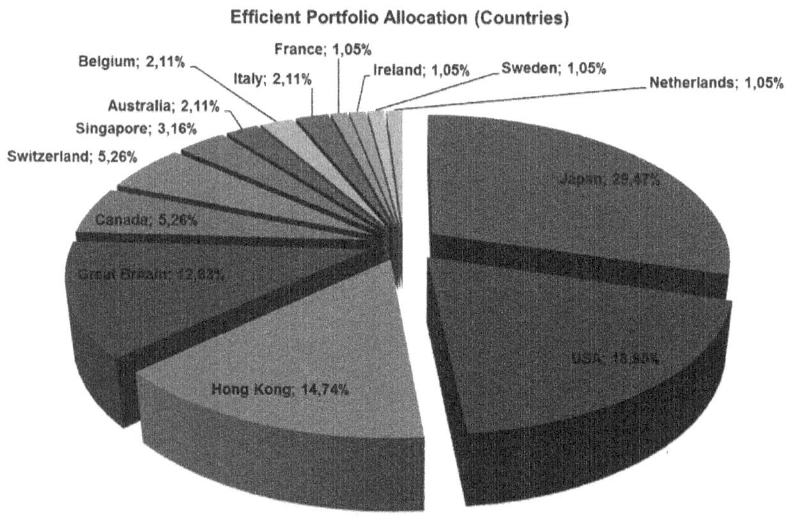


Figure 22: Efficient Country Allocation

# Chapter 5: Conclusions, Limitations & Outlook

## 5.1 Chapter Introduction

This final chapter answers the research questions which have been established in the beginning of this dissertation. Also the limitations of this study are outlined. The chapter finishes with suggestions for further research.

## 5.2 Conclusion

To reach the overall aim of this dissertation, the construction of a portfolio which earns higher returns by simultaneously lower systematic risk than the market portfolio, four research questions have been established.

- Is it possible to determine differences among the international stock markets regarding the beta-return relationship?

The answers to this question contribute further knowledge about international stock markets. Furthermore, the findings enable private and institutional investors who are interested in the optimisation of their portfolio structure. The author discovered that most of the previous research undertaken in this field was limited to single countries. By reviewing a huge number of academic articles it also came to light that research was subject to biases especially on how data was gathered (data snooping) or on how it was generated (e.g. calculations of beta).

To answer the first research question the Global Market has been analysed by using a comprehensive (1,800 stocks) and inherently consistent proxy. The data was gathered from a Professional Terminal by Bloomberg L.P., a leading, internationally accepted provider of financial data. Furthermore, the Global 1800 index allowed for a valid investigation across 24 countries. It came to light that US stocks account for

29.3% of the index in April 2011 which validates the findings of Odien & Solnik (1993) and invalidates the findings of studies using single country indices as a market proxy. This study found proof that the importance of countries within the Global Market is quite stable over time. Furthermore, it reflects that China is still a market of the future. This derives from the growing importance of the Hong Kong market as most of the listed companies are headquartered in China.

In general, the univariate analysis indicates only small time-varying betas. In the representative cross-section (except inefficient markets like Greece), it has been proven that a decrease in beta risk is followed by lower returns and therefore the attributed beta-return relationship remains quite stable over time. On the other hand, remarkable differences were found between the international stock markets regarding this relationship. This is foremost explained by the comparative advantages of the individual countries figured out during this study. In addition, the differences regarding the risk-return efficiency can be quantified by implementing a beta-return ratio.

- Do industry-sector-specific differences exist with regard to the beta-return relationship?

As STOXX Ltd., the provider of the proxy index also allows for an investigation across industries, it was possible to give important and valid evidence about differences between 19 supersectors. First of all, it is recognisable that the Global Market shows a relatively homogenous allocation of supersectors. Only the supersector "Industrial Goods & Services" stands out in its importance as it accounts for 14.89% while the majority proportions between 6.61% ("Technology") and 4.11% ("Chemicals"). Similar to the findings about countries regarding the time-variation of beta, the systematic risk of a supersector is rather stable over time. Only in cases of natural disasters or other economic incidents the betas vary more intensively.

So, to answer the secondary research question, the differences between supersectors are quite serious in regards to the beta-return relationship. Interestingly, some sectors show a quite efficient risk-return relation like "Telecommunications", "Chemicals" and "Food &Beverages" which are steadily able to outperform the market while others, like the three sectors of the financial industry and "Construction & Materials", are steadily risk-return inefficient. These differences have been quantified by using the beta-return ratio.

- What are the implications for an effective and efficient equity asset allocation?

To build an effective and efficient portfolio it can be concluded, that first of all investments should be made in countries and sectors with the best beta-return ratio. To give evidence, three portfolios have been build which analysed the 95 top performers according to the categories highest risk, lowest positive beta and lowest positive risk-return ratio. The results demonstrate that the CAPM holds true as the highest beta stocks gained the highest returns while the low beta portfolio underperformed the Global Market. However, the major outcome and the answer to third research question is, that the third portfolio strongly outperformed the market in both periods April 2011 (excess returns: +33.40%) and November 2010 (+33.43%) while it was exposed to a dramatically lower systematic risk (April 2011: -0.53; November 2010: -0.62). As a result, a risk-return efficient portfolio is presented and the necessary and proper diversification across countries and supersectors was illustrated. Moreover, a diversification across countries is more important than a diversification across supersectors as but a few exceptions the countries are heavily dependent on one or two sectors.

- Is it effective to build a future-oriented investment strategy upon an ex-post beta/return analysis?

The examination, how many of the best performers in each category in November 2010 are still under the top 95 in April 2011 brought interesting but disappointing results. All of the predictors were not able to forecast future developments adequately. Anyhow, beta seems to be more stable than previous returns and beta-return ratios as 32.63% of the 2010-stocks were listed in the 2011-portfolio as well. Previous returns and the beta-return ratio both reached a strike rate of 26.32 which is by far not effective.

## 5.3 Limitations

The first limitation of this study is the data sample. Even though it allocates the most liquid stocks of the World's largest publicly listed companies, it is still not a perfect proxy for the World Stock market. The interesting emerging economies like the BRIC states, India and the Arabian markets are disregarded by this index. The Chinese market is only regarded by those companies listed in Hong Kong which does not sufficiently reflect this huge economy.

The second limitation is due to the cross-sectional analysis. While this gives a very good impression about the total market and allows for the explanation how external incidents affect supersectors and countries, it limits the statistical significance in regards to the predictability of stock behaviour.

A third limitation might lie in the literature review. Whilst all of the journals and books used for this work are of highest quality and helped to explain the findings of the analysis, the research about international and cross-sector stock market behaviour is scarce. Thus, it was quite difficult to compare findings and to validate them.

## 5.4 Future Research

Due to the limitations mentioned above further research is highly recommended. This work brought to light how a portfolio should be structured and diversified across countries and supersectors. While the data used in this work is based on yearly returns and corresponding betas, in further longitudinal studies, weekly or monthly data should be analysed. This should assist to find those stocks which are favourable within the supersectors and allow for a future-oriented investment strategy as this research question could not be answered satisfactorily. In addition, research conducted on a wider time period will make the findings even more valid.

Moreover, further research should focus on stock market anomalies from an international viewpoint. This should bring up more important information to verify und understand the findings of this dissertation. It should help to improve the predictability of stock returns. Due to the results of this works that betas are less time-varying than returns the power of the beta-return ratio will increase to find those market-outperformers which are stable and risk-return efficient over time.

# Appendices

## Appendix 1: Beta-Return Relations within supersectors – November 2010

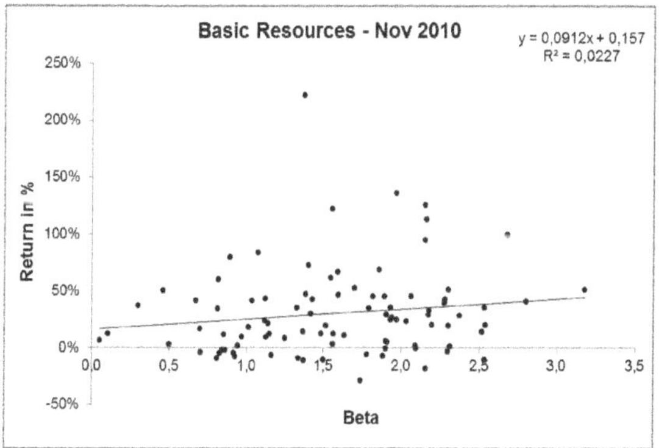


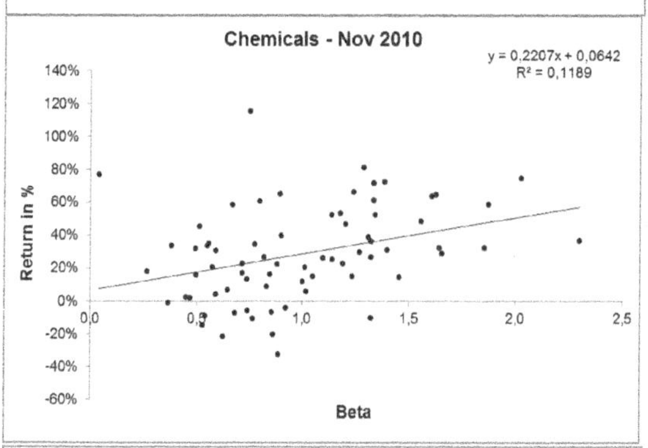


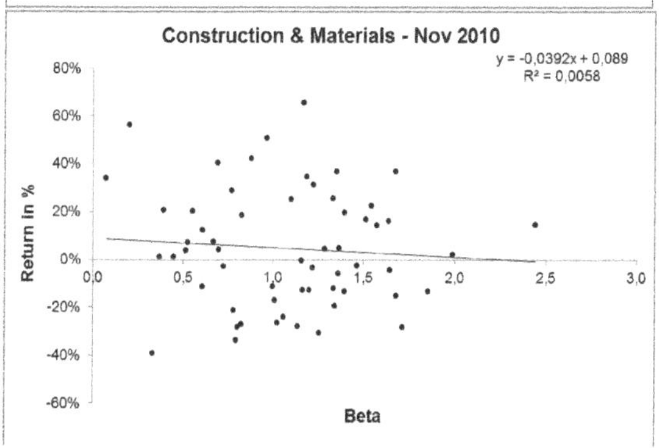

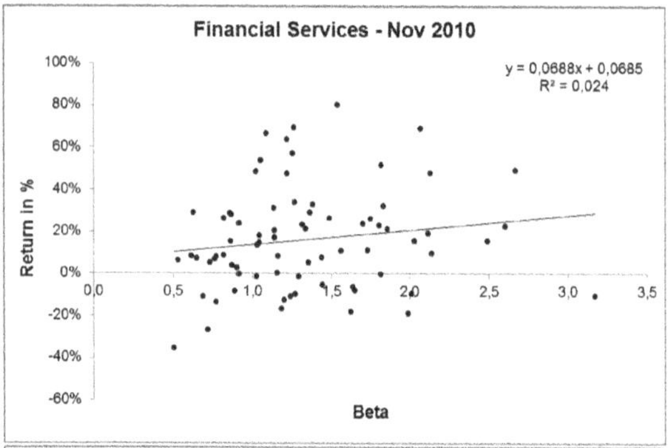
Financial Services - Nov 2010
y = 0,0688x + 0,0685
R² = 0,024
Return in %
Beta

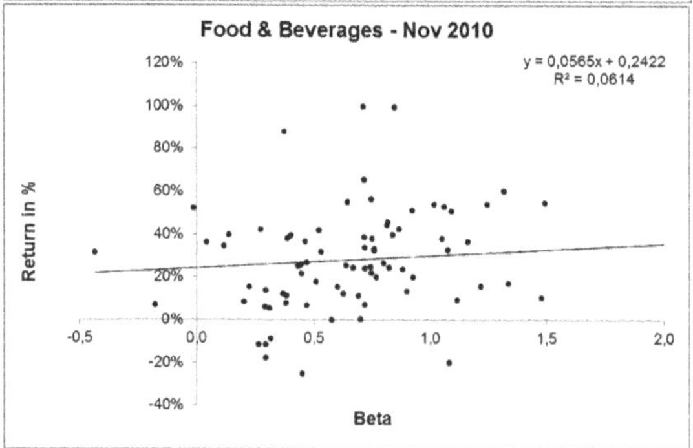
Food & Beverages - Nov 2010
y = 0,0565x + 0,2422
R² = 0,0614
Return in %
Beta

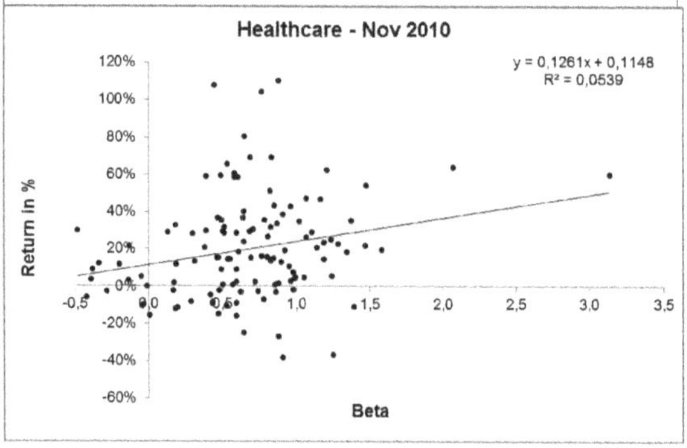
Healthcare - Nov 2010
y = 0,1261x + 0,1148
R² = 0,0539
Return in %
Beta

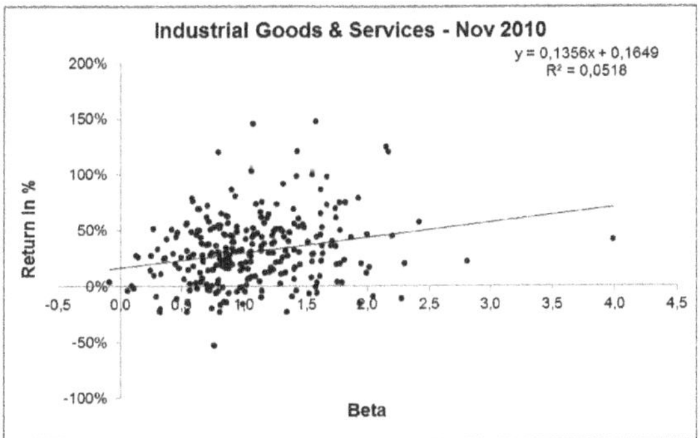
Industrial Goods & Services - Nov 2010
y = 0,1356x + 0,1649
R² = 0,0518
200%
150%
100%
50%
0%
-50%
-100%
Return in %
-0,5
0,0
0,5
1,0
1,5
2,0
2,5
3,0
3,5
4,0
4,5
Beta

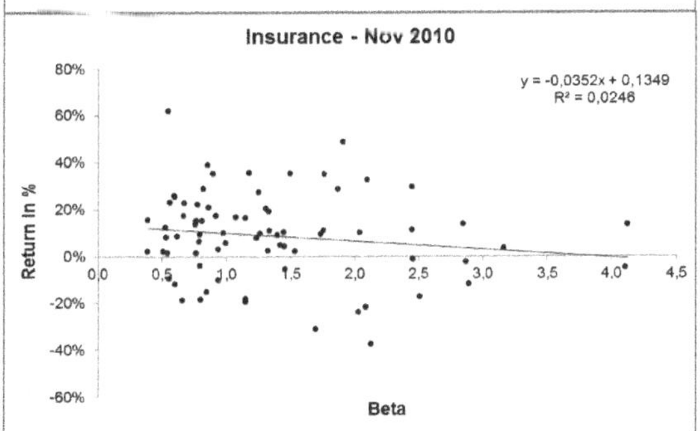
Insurance - Nov 2010
y = -0,0352x + 0,1349
R² = 0,0246
80%
60%
40%
20%
0%
-20%
-40%
-60%
Return in %
0,0
0,5
1,0
1,5
2,0
2,5
3,0
3,5
4,0
4,5
Beta

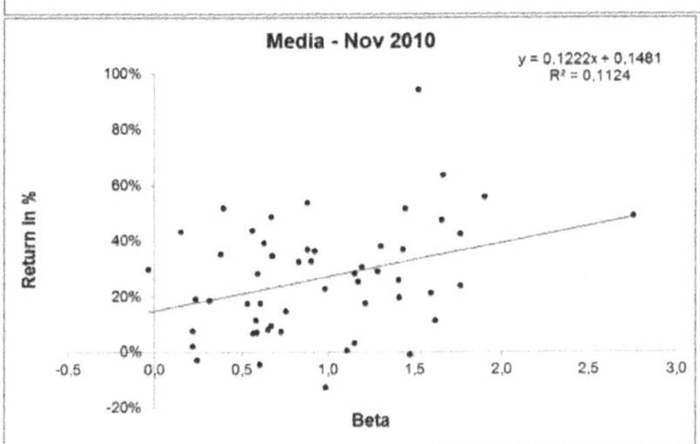
Media - Nov 2010
y = 0,1222x + 0,1481
R² = 0,1124
100%
80%
60%
40%
20%
0%
-20%
Return in %
-0,5
0,0
0,5
1,0
1,5
2,0
2,5
3,0
Beta

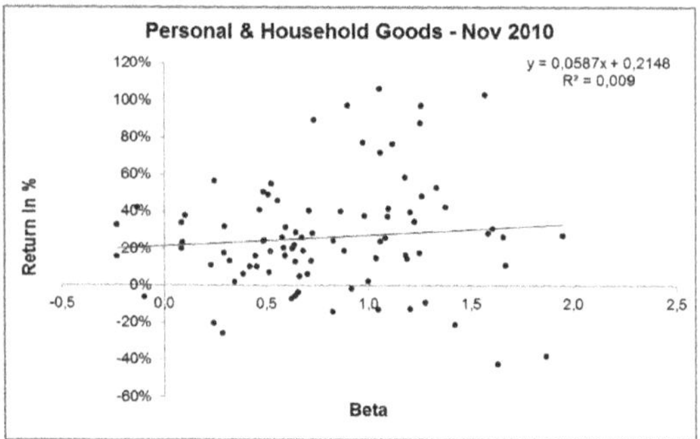
Personal & Household Goods - Nov 2010
y = 0,0587x + 0,2148
R² = 0,009
Return in %
Beta
120%
100%
80%
60%
40%
20%
0%
-20%
-40%
-60%
-0,5
0,0
0,5
1,0
1,5
2,0
2,5

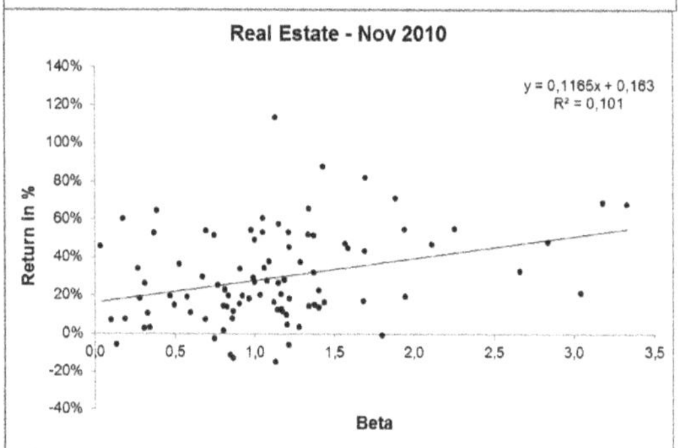
Real Estate - Nov 2010
y = 0,1165x + 0,163
R² = 0,101
Return in %
Beta
140%
120%
100%
80%
60%
40%
20%
0%
-20%
-40%
0,0
0,5
1,0
1,5
2,0
2,5
3,0
3,5

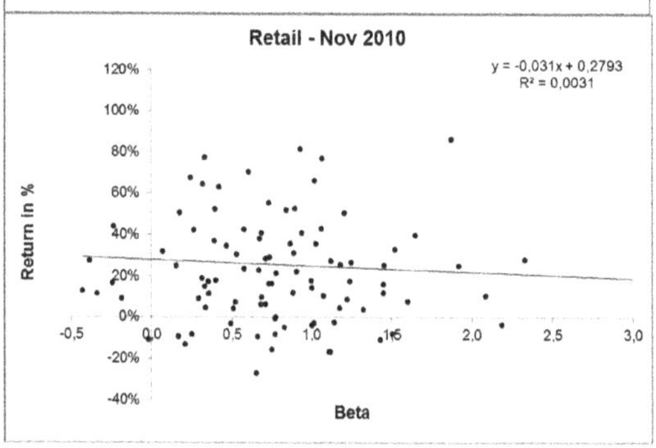
Retail - Nov 2010
y = -0,031x + 0,2793
R² = 0,0031
Return in %
Beta
120%
100%
80%
60%
40%
20%
0%
-20%
-40%
-0,5
0,0
0,5
1,0
1,5
2,0
2,5
3,0

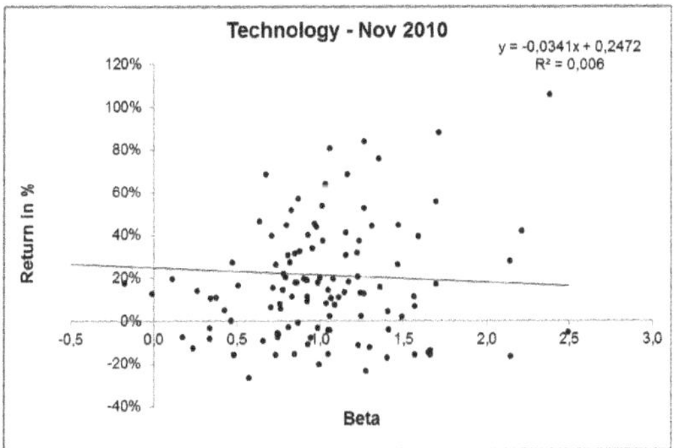
Technology - Nov 2010
y = -0,0341x + 0,2472
R² = 0,006
Return in %
120%
100%
80%
60%
40%
20%
0%
-20%
-40%
-0,5
0,0
0,5
1,0
1,5
2,0
2,5
3,0
Beta

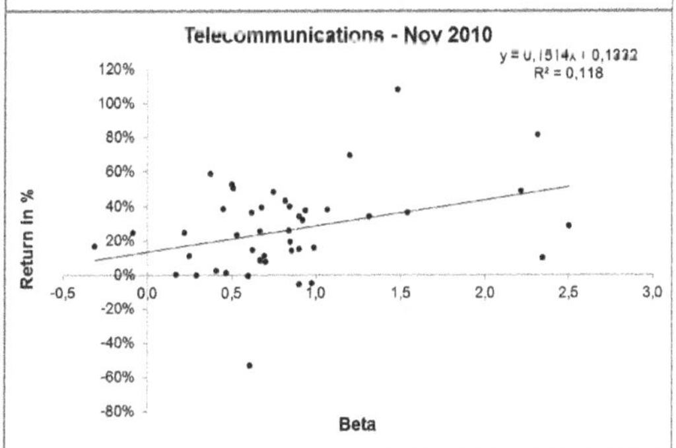
Telecommunications - Nov 2010
y = 0,1514x + 0,1332
R² = 0,118
Return in %
120%
100%
80%
60%
40%
20%
0%
-20%
-40%
-60%
-80%
-0,5
0,0
0,5
1,0
1,5
2,0
2,5
3,0
Beta

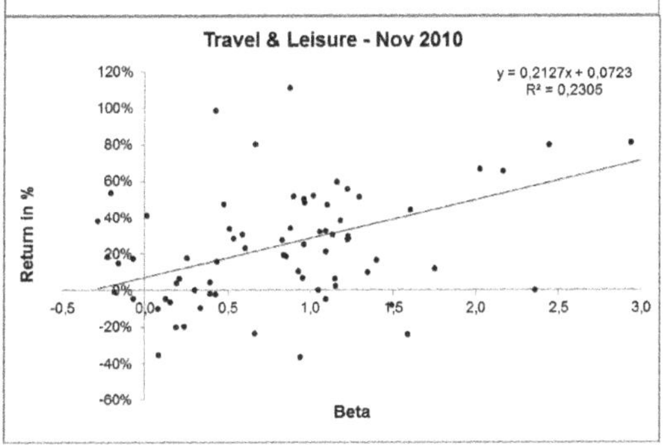
Travel & Leisure - Nov 2010
y = 0,2127x + 0,0723
R² = 0,2305
Return in %
120%
100%
80%
60%
40%
20%
0%
-20%
-40%
-60%
-0,5
0,0
0,5
1,0
1,5
2,0
2,5
3,0
Beta

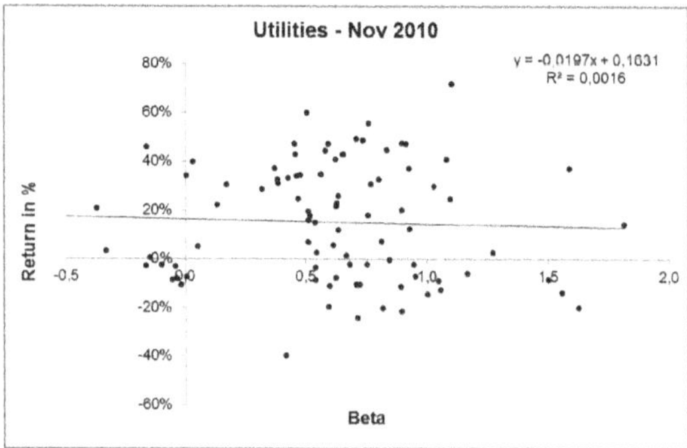
Utilities - Nov 2010
y = -0,0197x + 0,1631
R² = 0,0016
80%
60%
40%
20%
0%
-20%
-40%
-60%
-0,5
0,0
0,5
1,0
1,5
2,0
Return in %
Beta

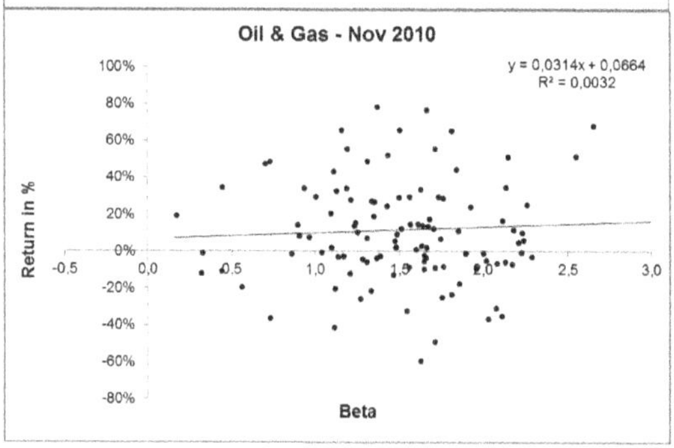
Oil & Gas - Nov 2010
y = 0,0314x + 0,0664
R² = 0,0032
100%
80%
60%
40%
20%
0%
-20%
-40%
-60%
-80%
-0,5
0,0
0,5
1,0
1,5
2,0
2,5
3,0
Return in %
Beta

# Appendix 2: Beta-Return Relations within supersectors – April 2011

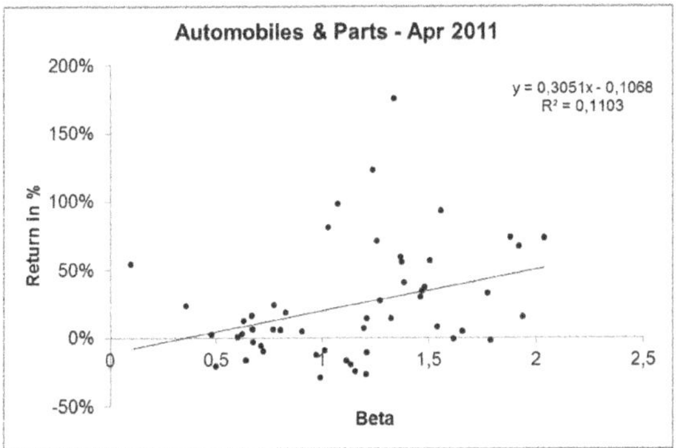


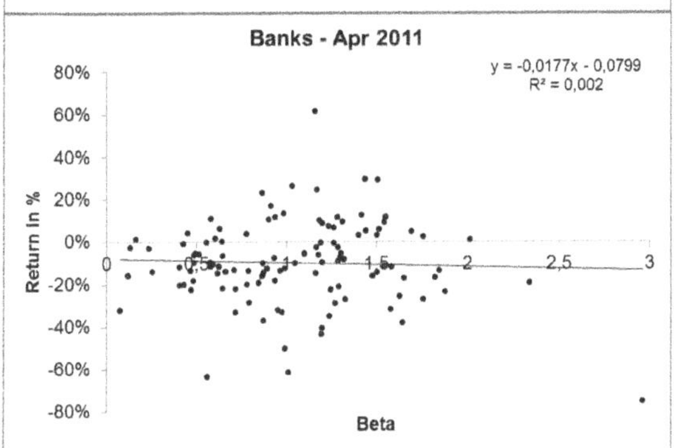


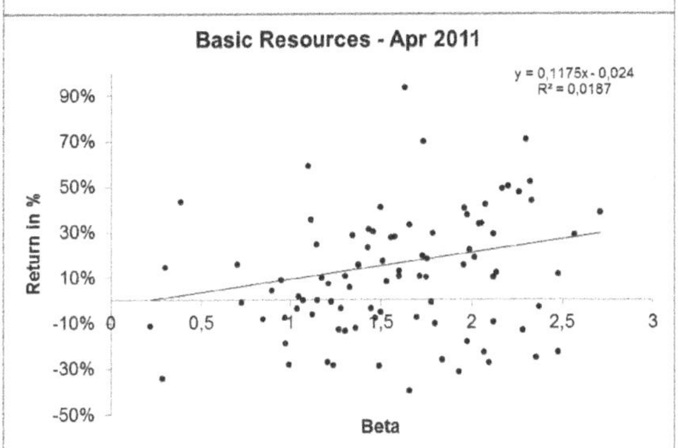

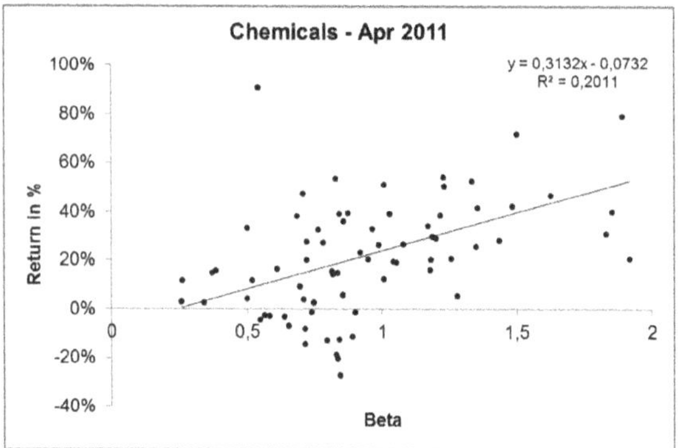
Chemicals - Apr 2011
y = 0,3132x - 0,0732
R² = 0,2011
100%
80%
60%
40%
20%
0%
-20%
-40%
Return in %
0
0,5
1
1,5
2
Beta

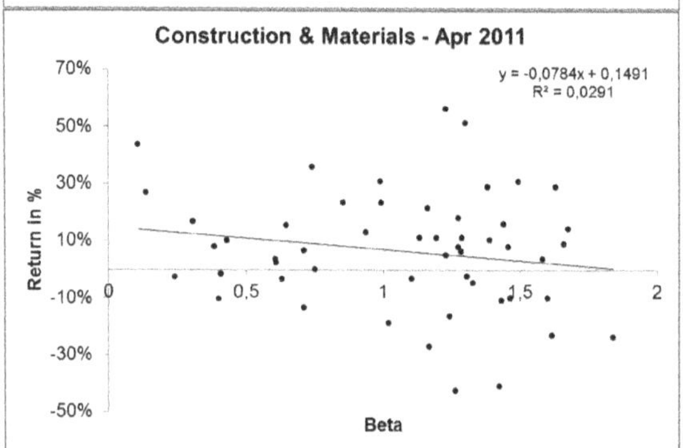
Construction & Materials - Apr 2011
y = -0,0784x + 0,1491
R² = 0,0291
70%
50%
30%
10%
-10%
-30%
-50%
Return in %
0
0,5
1
1,5
2
Beta

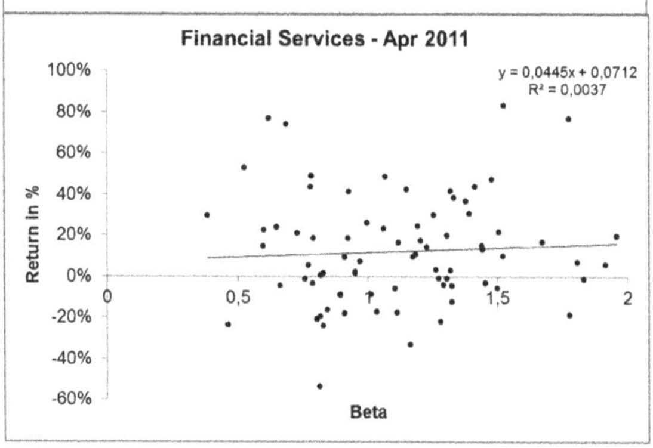
Financial Services - Apr 2011
y = 0,0445x + 0,0712
R² = 0,0037
100%
80%
60%
40%
20%
0%
-20%
-40%
-60%
Return in %
0
0,5
1
1,5
2
Beta

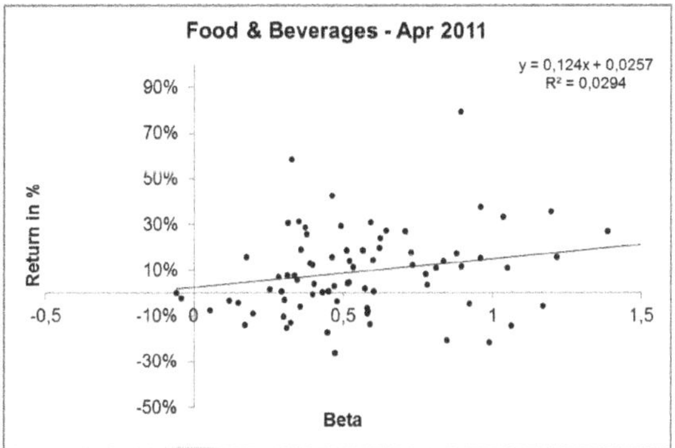
Food & Beverages - Apr 2011
y = 0,124x + 0,0257
R² = 0,0294
90%
70%
50%
30%
10%
-10%
-30%
-50%
Return in %
-0,5
0
0,5
1
1,5
Beta

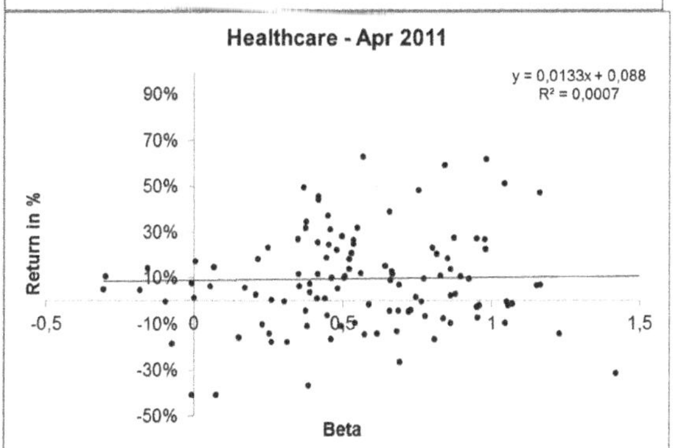
Healthcare - Apr 2011
y = 0,0133x + 0,088
R² = 0,0007
90%
70%
50%
30%
10%
-10%
-30%
-50%
Return in %
-0,5
0
0,5
1
1,5
Beta

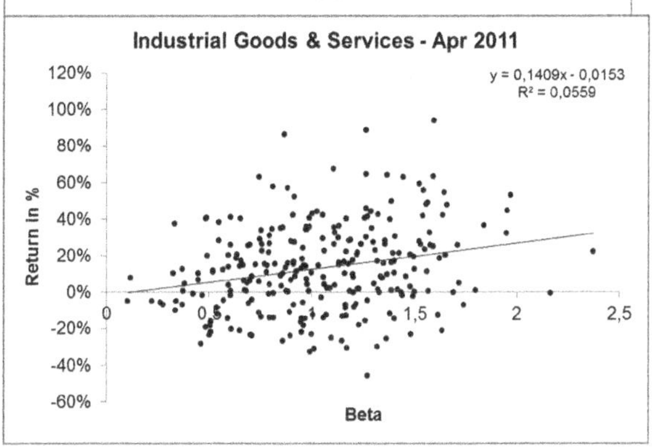
Industrial Goods & Services - Apr 2011
y = 0,1409x - 0,0153
R² = 0,0559
120%
100%
80%
60%
40%
20%
0%
-20%
-40%
-60%
Return in %
0
0,5
1
1,5
2
2,5
Beta

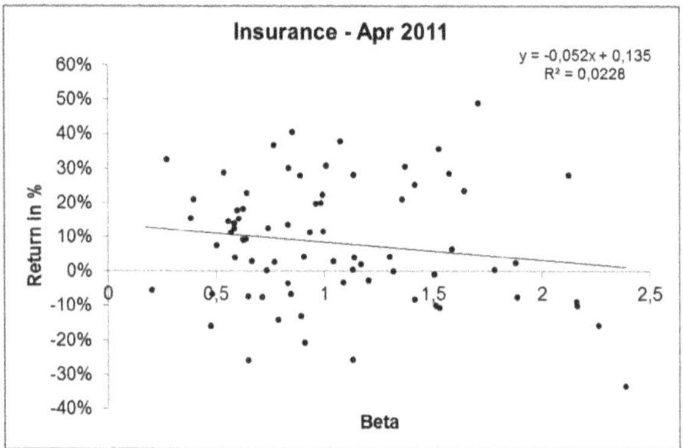
Insurance - Apr 2011
y = -0,052x + 0,135
R² = 0,0228
Return in %
Beta
60%
50%
40%
30%
20%
10%
0%
-10%
-20%
-30%
-40%
0
0,5
1
1,5
2
2,5

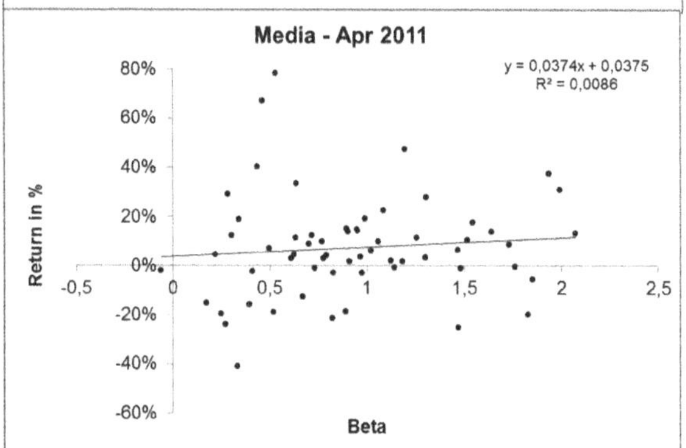
Media - Apr 2011
y = 0,0374x + 0,0375
R² = 0,0086
Return in %
Beta
80%
60%
40%
20%
0%
-20%
-40%
-60%
-0,5
0
0,5
1
1,5
2
2,5

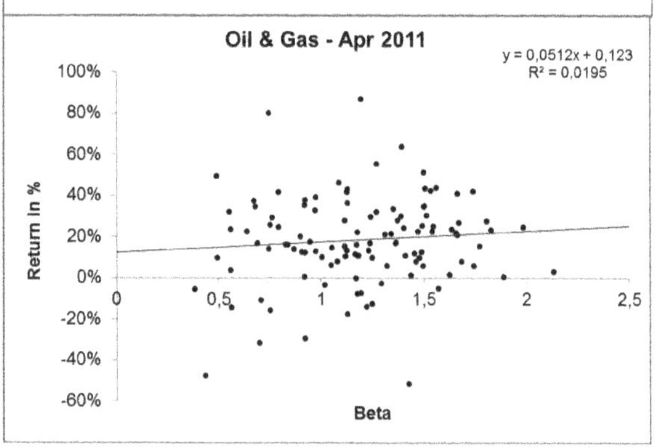
Oil & Gas - Apr 2011
y = 0,0512x + 0,123
R² = 0,0195
Return in %
Beta
100%
80%
60%
40%
20%
0%
-20%
-40%
-60%
0
0,5
1
1,5
2
2,5

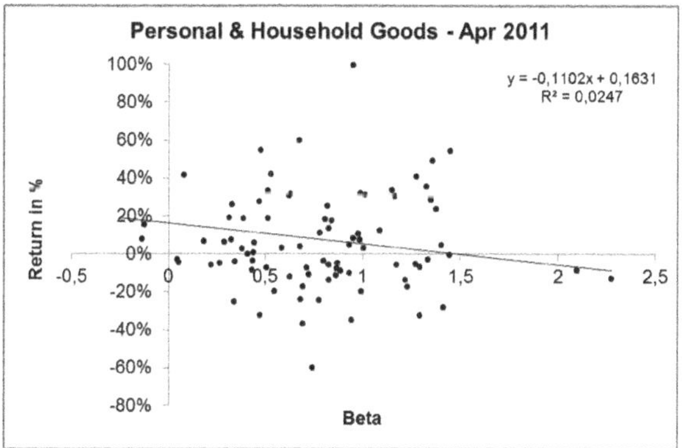
Personal & Household Goods - Apr 2011
y = -0,1102x + 0,1631
R² = 0,0247
Return in %
Beta
100%
80%
60%
40%
20%
0%
-20%
-40%
-60%
-80%
-0,5
0
0,5
1
1,5
2
2,5

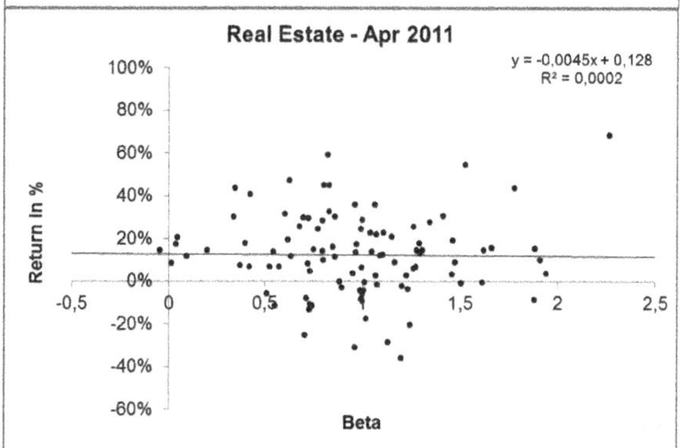
Real Estate - Apr 2011
y = -0,0045x + 0,128
R² = 0,0002
Return in %
Beta
100%
80%
60%
40%
20%
0%
-20%
-40%
-60%
-0,5
0
0,5
1
1,5
2
2,5

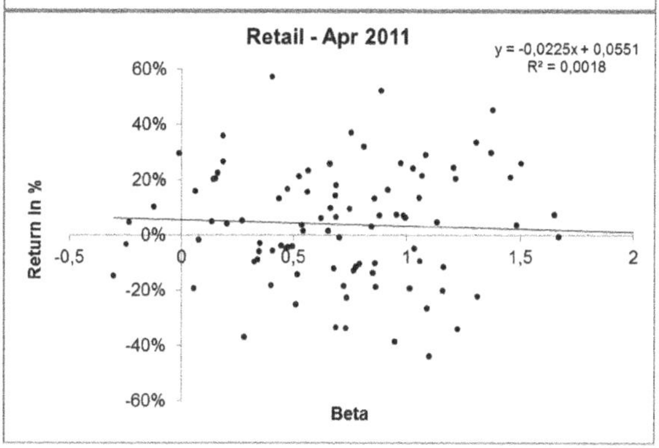
Retail - Apr 2011
y = -0,0225x + 0,0551
R² = 0,0018
Return in %
Beta
60%
40%
20%
0%
-20%
-40%
-60%
-0,5
0
0,5
1
1,5
2

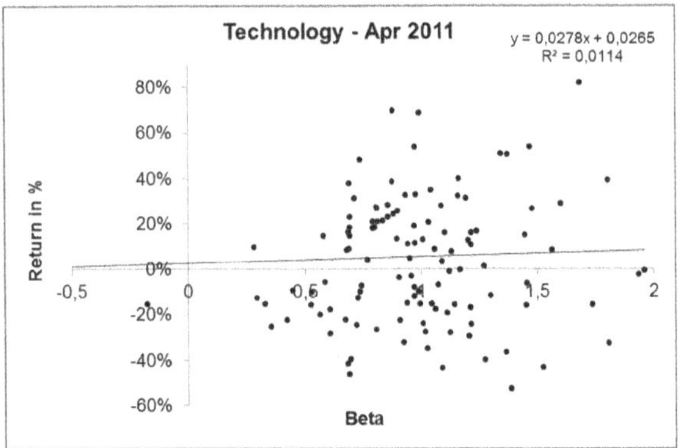
Technology - Apr 2011
y = 0,0278x + 0,0265
R² = 0,0114
80%
60%
40%
20%
0%
-20%
-40%
-60%
-0,5
0
0,5
1
1,5
2
Return in %
Beta

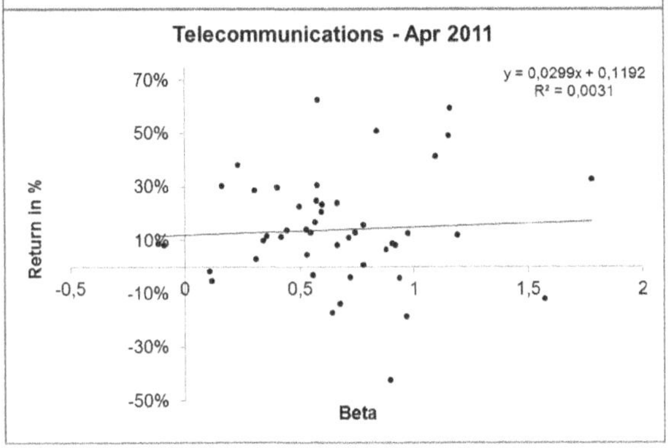
Telecommunications - Apr 2011
y = 0,0299x + 0,1192
R² = 0,0031
70%
50%
30%
10%
-10%
-30%
-50%
-0,5
0
0,5
1
1,5
2
Return in %
Beta

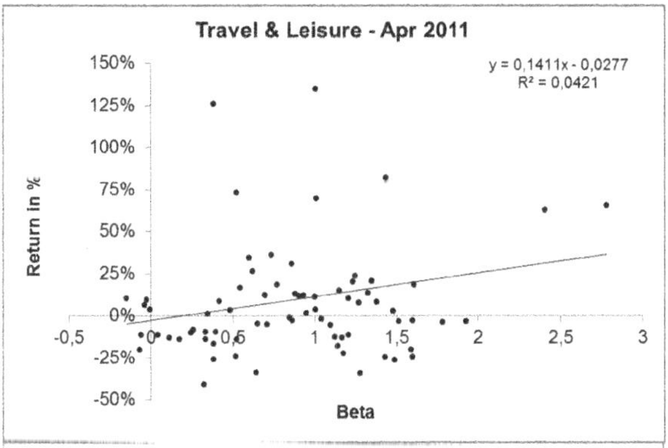
Travel & Leisure - Apr 2011
y = 0,1411x - 0,0277
R² = 0,0421
150%
125%
100%
75%
50%
25%
0%
-25%
-50%
Return in %
-0,5
0
0,5
1
1,5
2
2,5
3
Beta

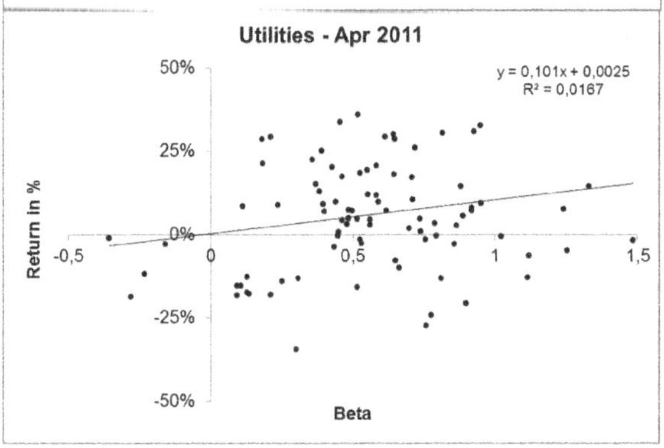
Utilities - Apr 2011
y = 0,101x + 0,0025
R² = 0,0167
50%
25%
0%
-25%
-50%
Return in %
-0,5
0
0,5
1
1,5
Beta

## Appendix 3: Beta-Return Relations within countries – November 2010

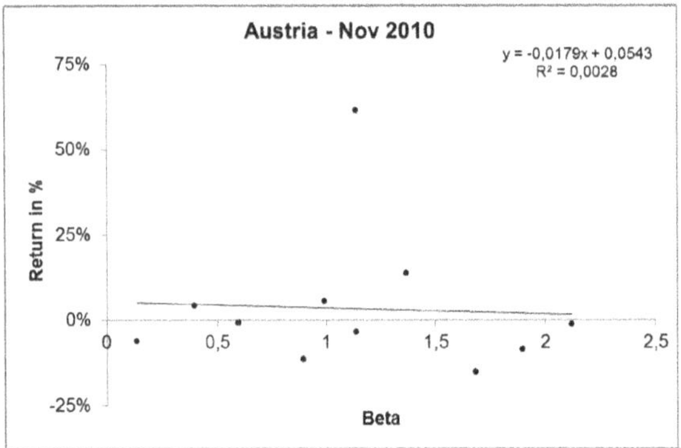


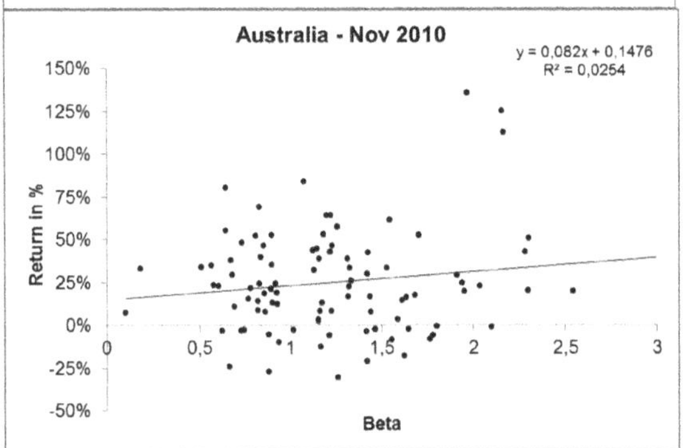


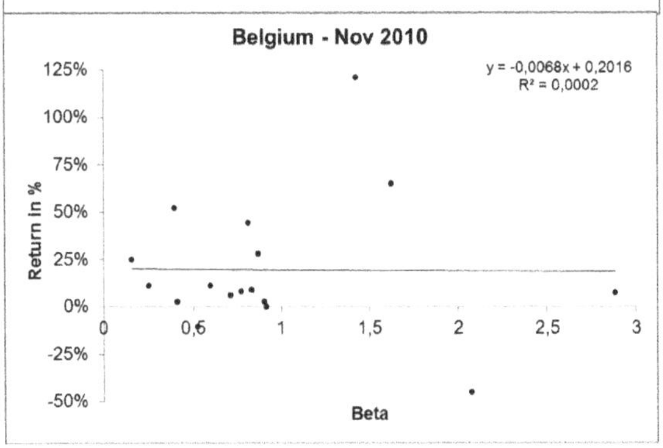

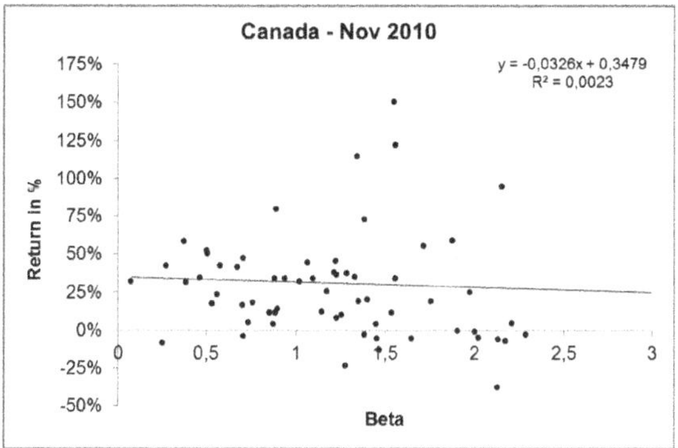
Canada - Nov 2010
y = -0,0326x + 0,3479
R² = 0,0023
175%
150%
125%
100%
75%
50%
25%
0%
-25%
-50%
Return in %
0
0,5
1
1,5
2
2,5
3
Beta

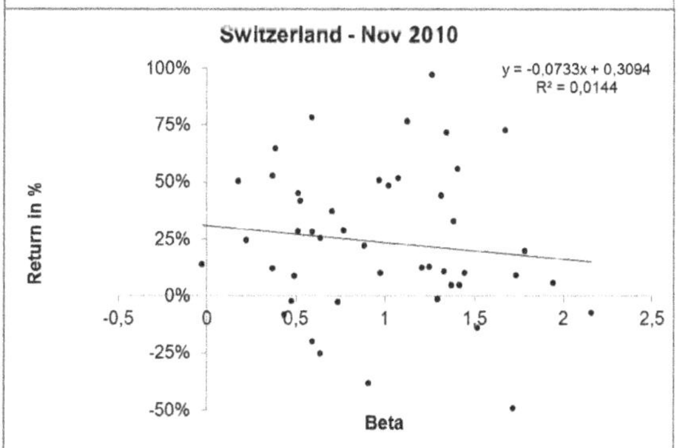
Switzerland - Nov 2010
y = -0,0733x + 0,3094
R² = 0,0144
100%
75%
50%
25%
0%
-25%
-50%
Return in %
-0,5
0
0,5
1
1,5
2
2,5
Beta

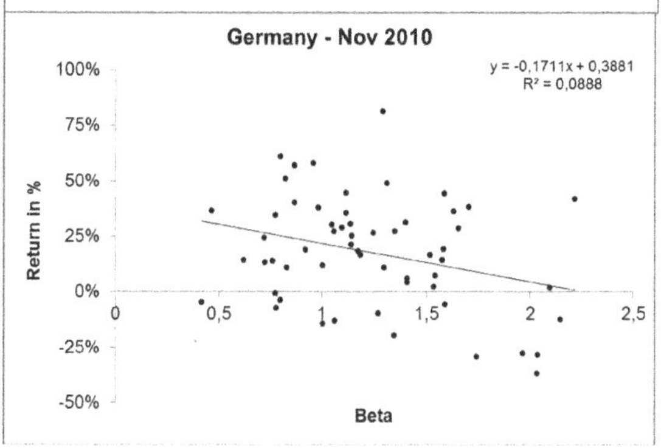
Germany - Nov 2010
y = -0,1711x + 0,3881
R² = 0,0888
100%
75%
50%
25%
0%
-25%
-50%
Return in %
0
0,5
1
1,5
2
2,5
Beta

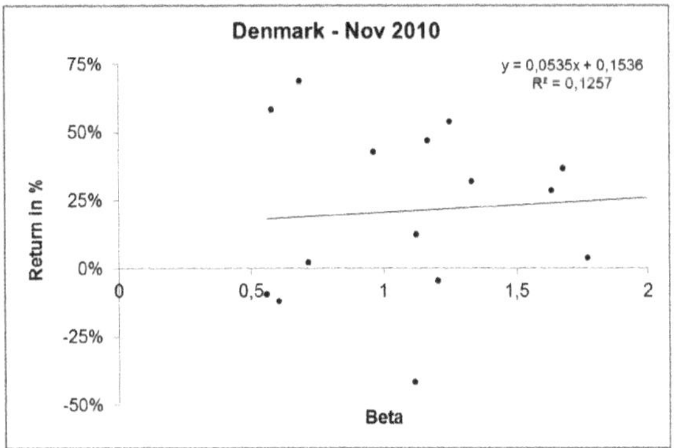
Denmark - Nov 2010
y = 0,0535x + 0,1536
R² = 0,1257
75%
50%
25%
0%
-25%
-50%
Return in %
0
0,5
1
1,5
2
Beta

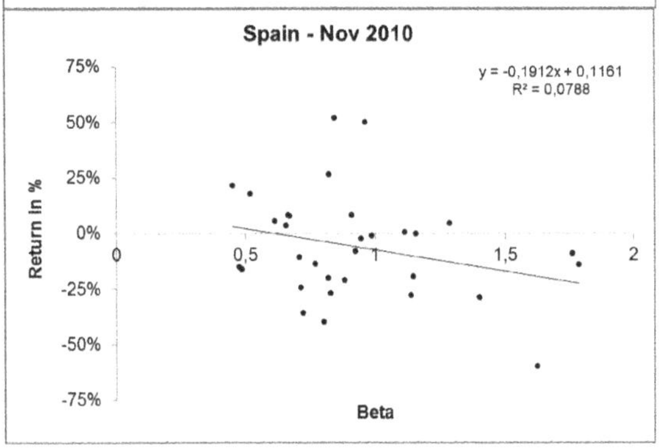
Spain - Nov 2010
y = -0,1912x + 0,1161
R² = 0,0788
75%
50%
25%
0%
-25%
-50%
-75%
Return in %
0
0,5
1
1,5
2
Beta

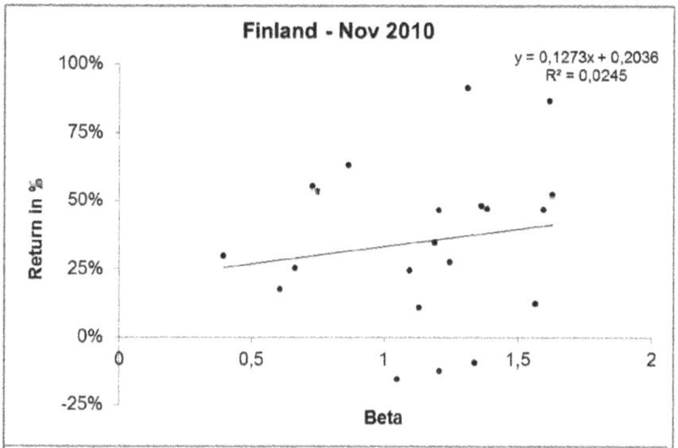
Finland - Nov 2010
y = 0,1273x + 0,2036
R² = 0,0245
100%
75%
50%
25%
0%
-25%
Return in %
0
0,5
1
1,5
2
Beta

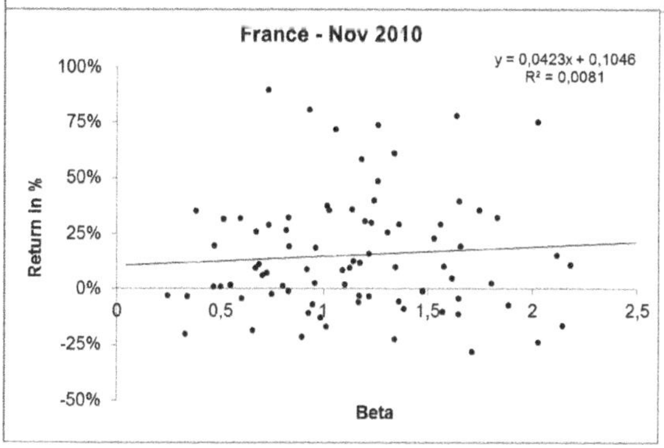
France - Nov 2010
y = 0,0423x + 0,1046
R² = 0,0081
100%
75%
50%
25%
0%
-25%
-50%
Return in %
0
0,5
1
1,5
2
2,5
Beta

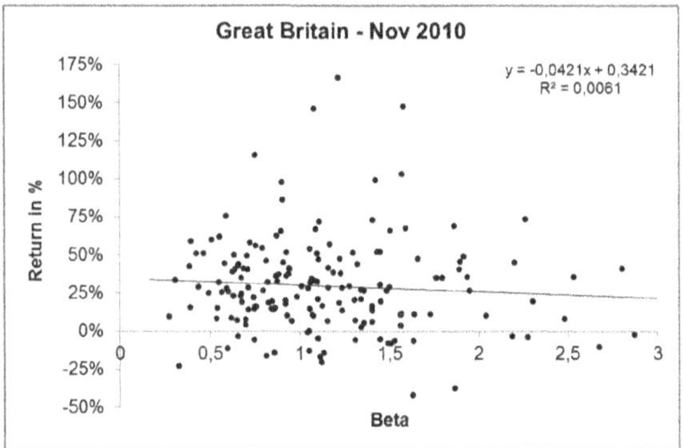
Great Britain - Nov 2010
y = -0,0421x + 0,3421
R² = 0,0061
175%
150%
125%
100%
75%
50%
25%
0%
-25%
-50%
0
0,5
1
1,5
2
2,5
3
Return in %
Beta

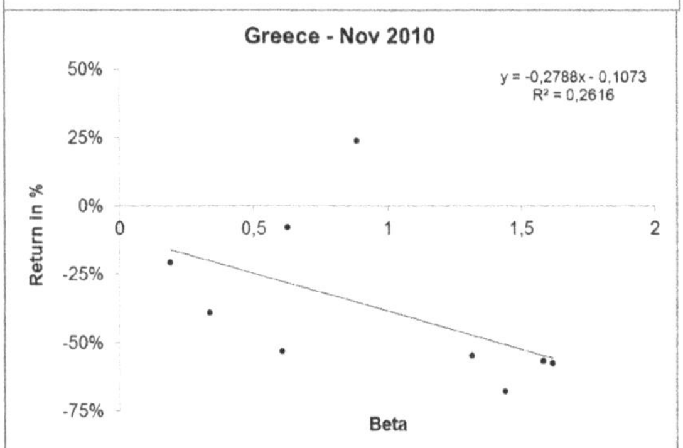
Greece - Nov 2010
y = -0,2788x - 0,1073
R² = 0,2616
50%
25%
0%
-25%
-50%
-75%
0
0,5
1
1,5
2
Return in %
Beta

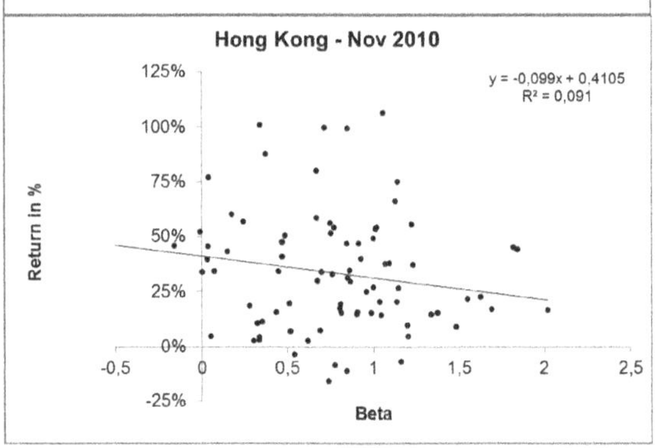
Hong Kong - Nov 2010
y = -0,099x + 0,4105
R² = 0,091
125%
100%
75%
50%
25%
0%
-25%
-0,5
0
0,5
1
1,5
2
2,5
Return in %
Beta

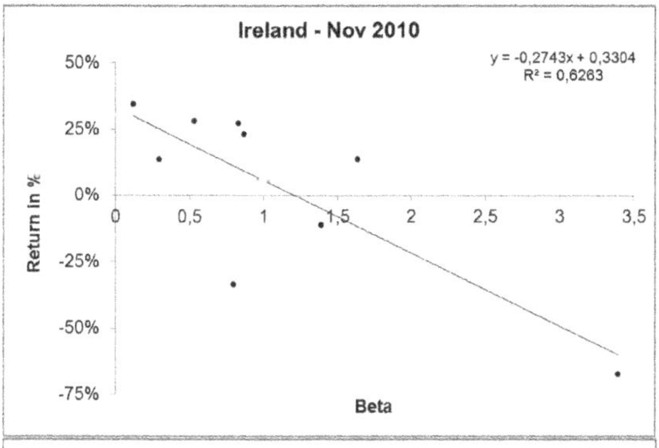
Ireland - Nov 2010
y = -0,2743x + 0,3304
R² = 0,6263
50%
25%
0%
-25%
-50%
-75%
0
0,5
1
1,5
2
2,5
3
3,5
Return in %
Beta

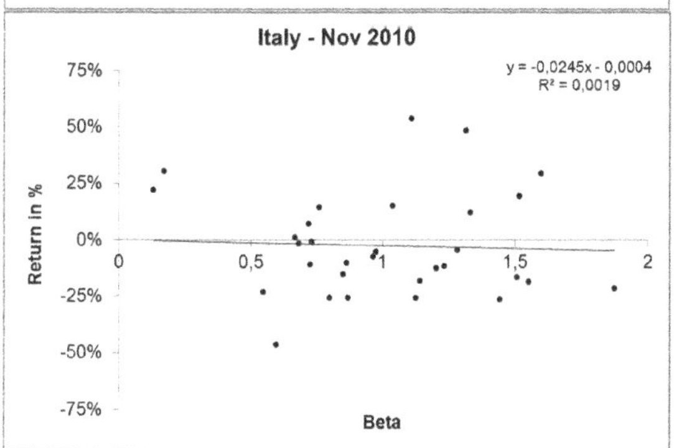
Italy - Nov 2010
y = -0,0245x - 0,0004
R² = 0,0019
75%
50%
25%
0%
-25%
-50%
-75%
0
0,5
1
1,5
2
Return in %
Beta

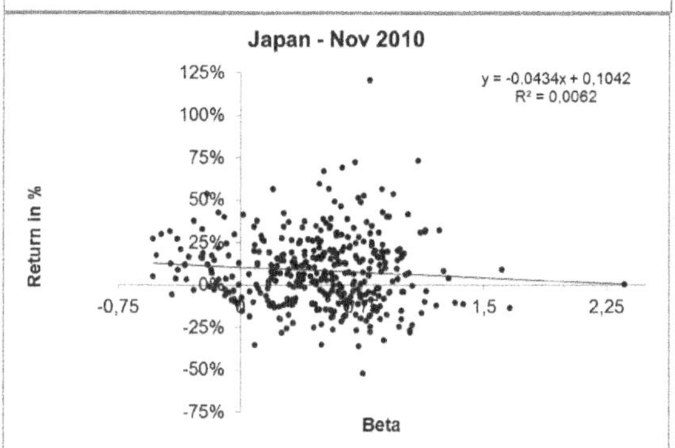
Japan - Nov 2010
y = -0,0434x + 0,1042
R² = 0,0062
125%
100%
75%
50%
25%
0%
-25%
-50%
-75%
-0,75
1,5
2,25
Return in %
Beta

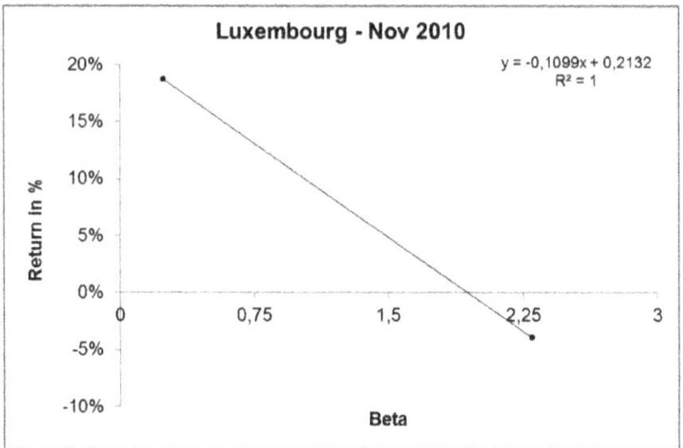
Luxembourg - Nov 2010
y = -0,1099x + 0,2132
R² = 1
20%
15%
10%
5%
0%
-5%
-10%
Return in %
0
0,75
1,5
2,25
3
Beta

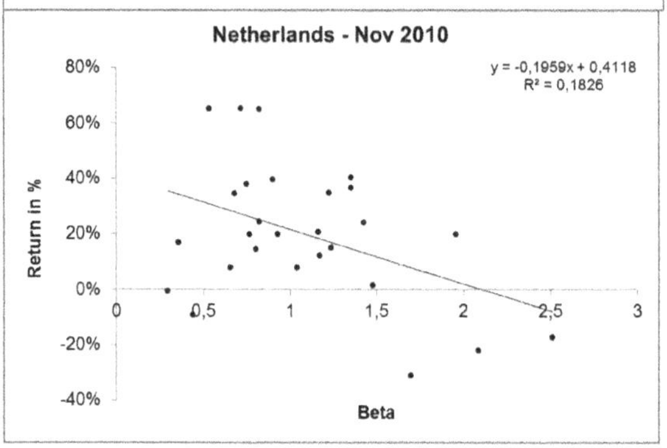
Netherlands - Nov 2010
y = -0,1959x + 0,4118
R² = 0,1826
80%
60%
40%
20%
0%
-20%
-40%
Return in %
0
0,5
1
1,5
2
2,5
3
Beta

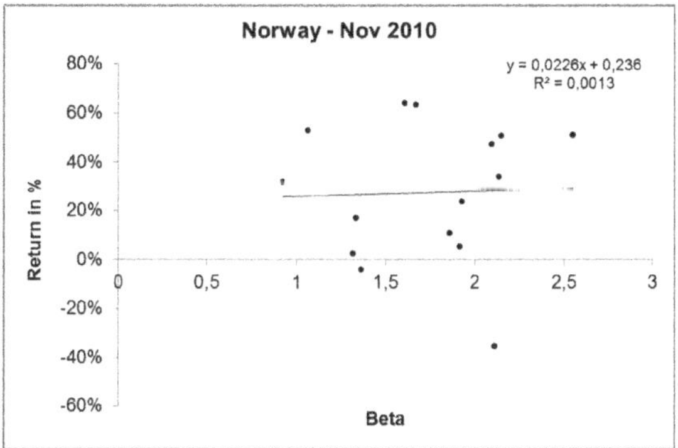
Norway - Nov 2010
y = 0,0226x + 0,236
R² = 0,0013
80%
60%
40%
20%
0%
-20%
-40%
-60%
0
0,5
1
1,5
2
2,5
3
Return in %
Beta

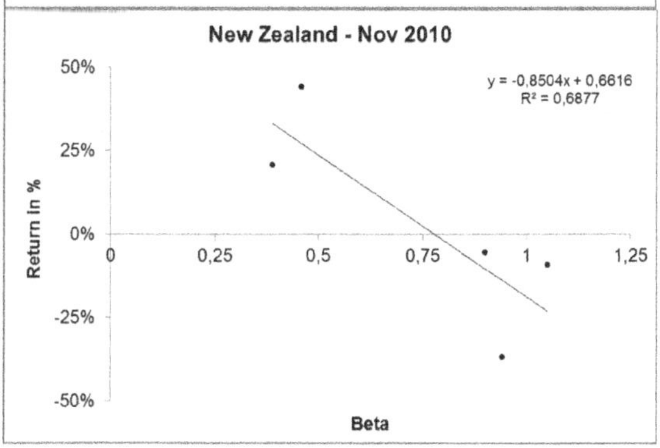
New Zealand - Nov 2010
y = -0,8504x + 0,6616
R² = 0,6877
50%
25%
0%
-25%
-50%
0
0,25
0,5
0,75
1
1,25
Return in %
Beta

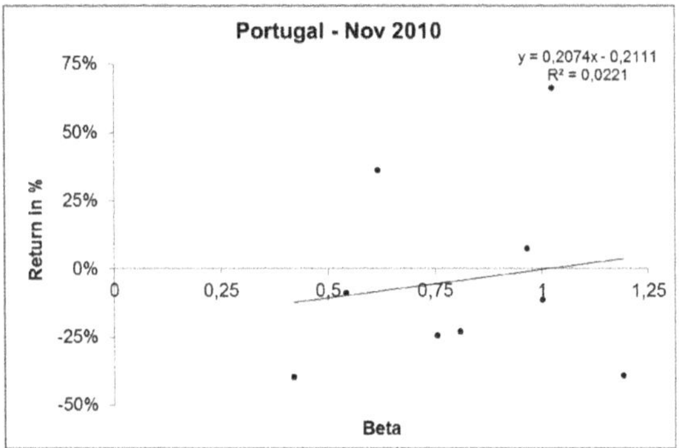
Portugal - Nov 2010
y = 0,2074x - 0,2111
R² = 0,0221
75%
50%
25%
0%
-25%
-50%
Return in %
0
0,25
0,5
0,75
1
1,25
Beta

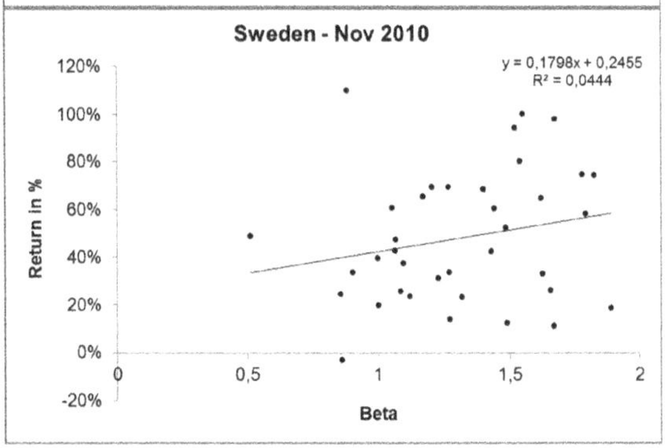
Sweden - Nov 2010
y = 0,1798x + 0,2455
R² = 0,0444
120%
100%
80%
60%
40%
20%
0%
-20%
Return in %
0
0,5
1
1,5
2
Beta

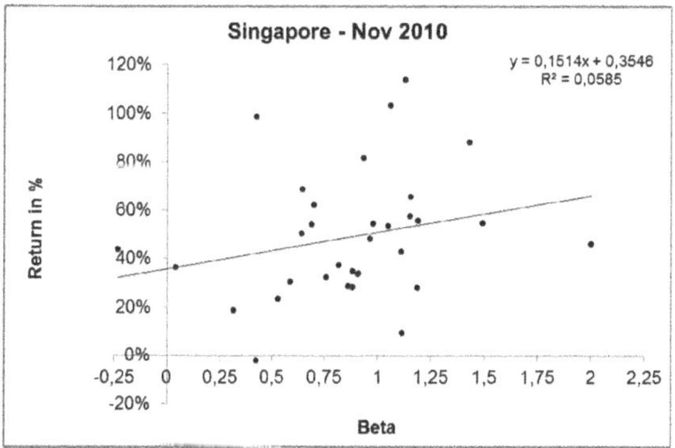
Singapore - Nov 2010
y = 0,1514x + 0,3546
R² = 0,0585
Return in %
120%
100%
80%
60%
40%
20%
0%
-20%
-0,25
0
0,25
0,5
0,75
1
1,25
1,5
1,75
2
2,25
Beta

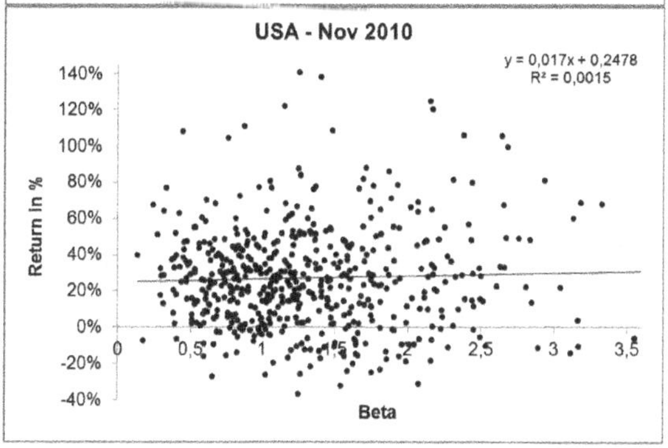
USA - Nov 2010
y = 0,017x + 0,2478
R² = 0,0015
Return in %
140%
120%
100%
80%
60%
40%
20%
0%
-20%
-40%
0
0,5
1
1,5
2
2,5
3
3,5
Beta

## Appendix 4: Beta-Return Relations within countries – April 2011

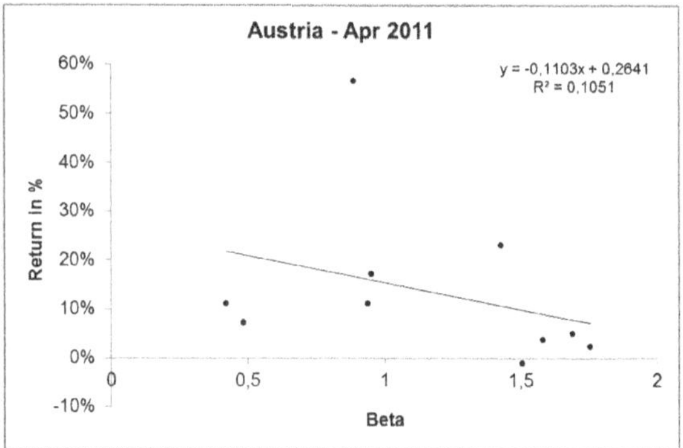


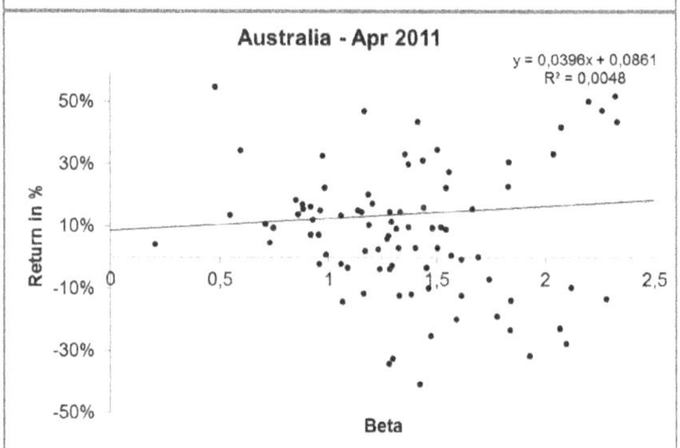


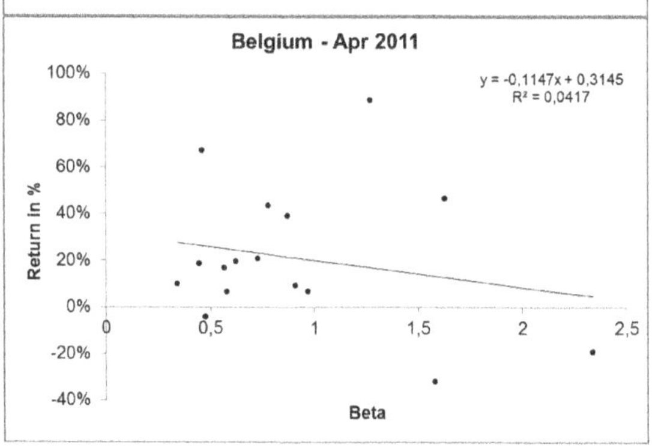

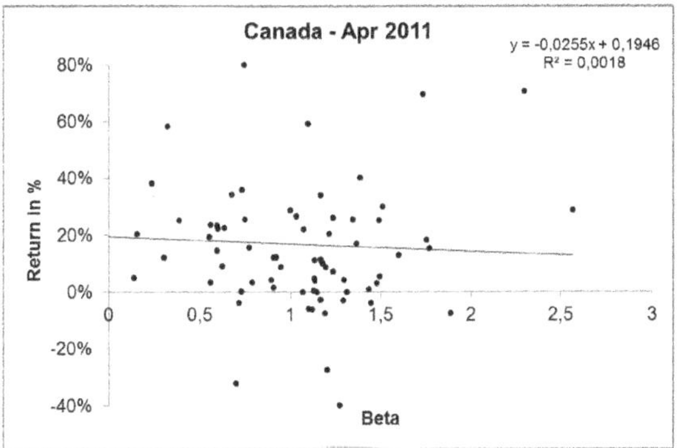
Canada - Apr 2011
y = -0,0255x + 0,1946
R² = 0,0018
80%
60%
40%
20%
0%
-20%
-40%
Return in %
0
0,5
1
1,5
2
2,5
3
Beta

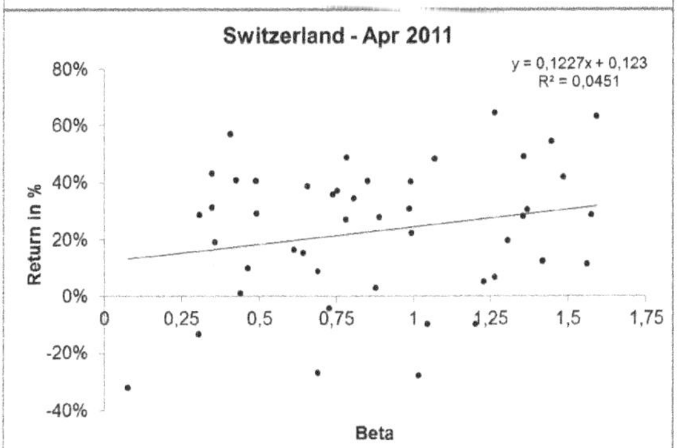
Switzerland - Apr 2011
y = 0,1227x + 0,123
R² = 0,0451
80%
60%
40%
20%
0%
-20%
-40%
Return in %
0
0,25
0,5
0,75
1
1,25
1,5
1,75
Beta

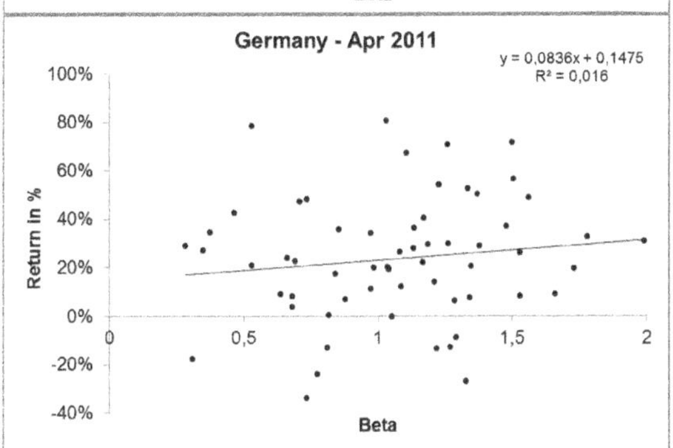
Germany - Apr 2011
y = 0,0836x + 0,1475
R² = 0,016
100%
80%
60%
40%
20%
0%
-20%
-40%
Return in %
0
0,5
1
1,5
2
Beta

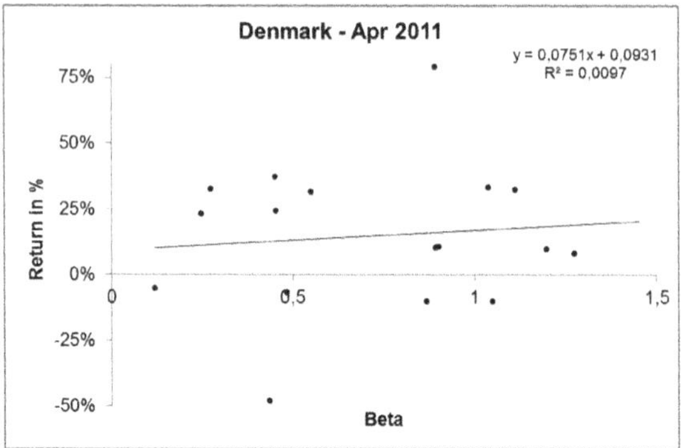
Denmark - Apr 2011
y = 0,0751x + 0,0931
R² = 0,0097
75%
50%
25%
0%
-25%
-50%
Return in %
0
0,5
1
1,5
Beta

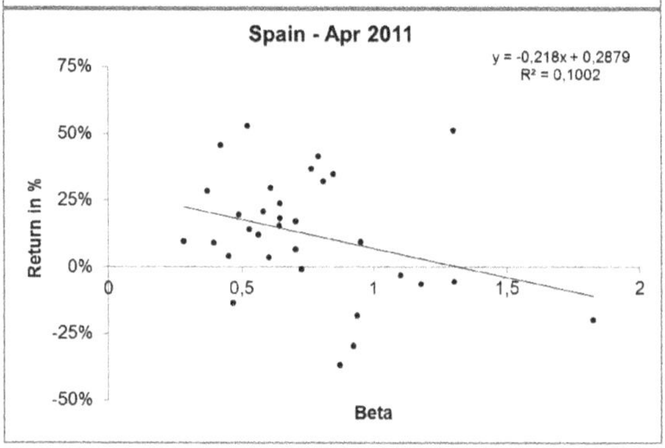
Spain - Apr 2011
y = -0,218x + 0,2879
R² = 0,1002
75%
50%
25%
0%
-25%
-50%
Return in %
0
0,5
1
1,5
2
Beta

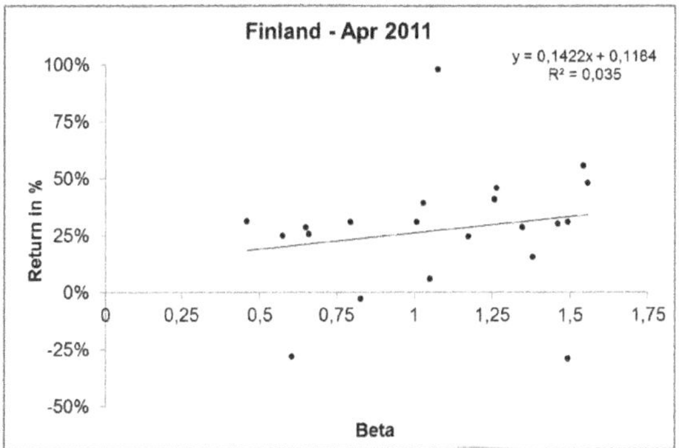
Finland - Apr 2011
y = 0,1422x + 0,1184
R² = 0,035
100%
75%
50%
25%
0%
-25%
-50%
Return in %
0
0,25
0,5
0,75
1
1,25
1,5
1,75
Beta

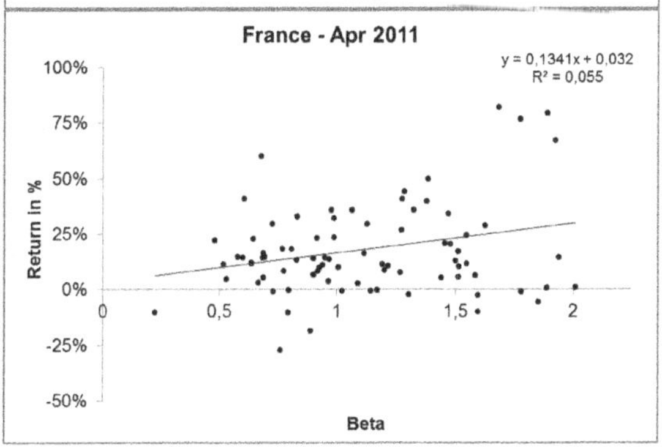
France - Apr 2011
y = 0,1341x + 0,032
R² = 0,055
100%
75%
50%
25%
0%
-25%
-50%
Return in %
0
0,5
1
1,5
2
Beta

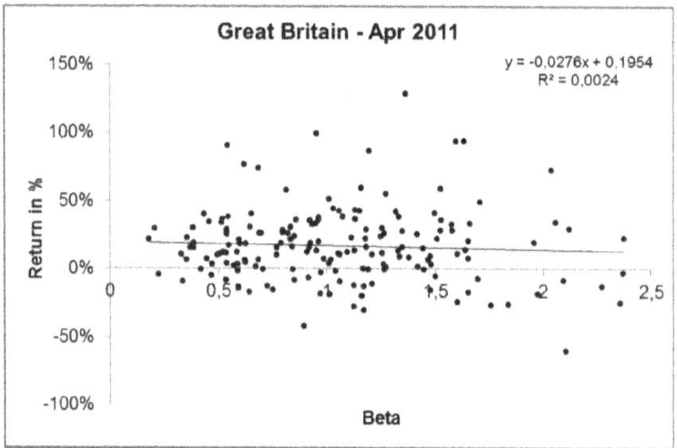
Great Britain - Apr 2011
y = -0,0276x + 0,1954
R² = 0,0024
150%
100%
50%
0%
-50%
-100%
Return in %
0
0,5
1
1,5
2
2,5
Beta

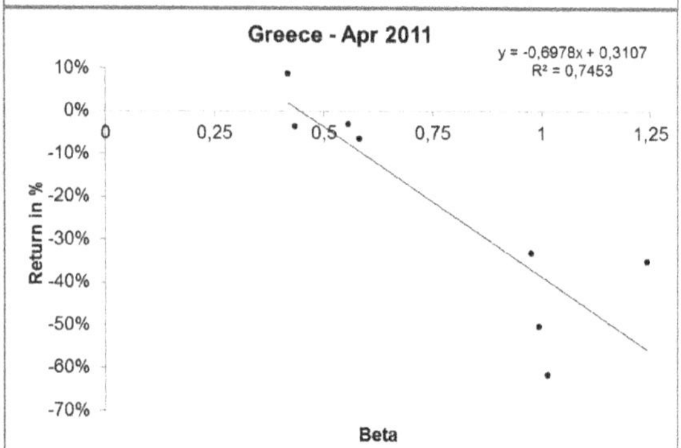
Greece - Apr 2011
y = -0,6978x + 0,3107
R² = 0,7453
10%
0%
-10%
-20%
-30%
-40%
-50%
-60%
-70%
Return in %
0
0,25
0,5
0,75
1
1,25
Beta

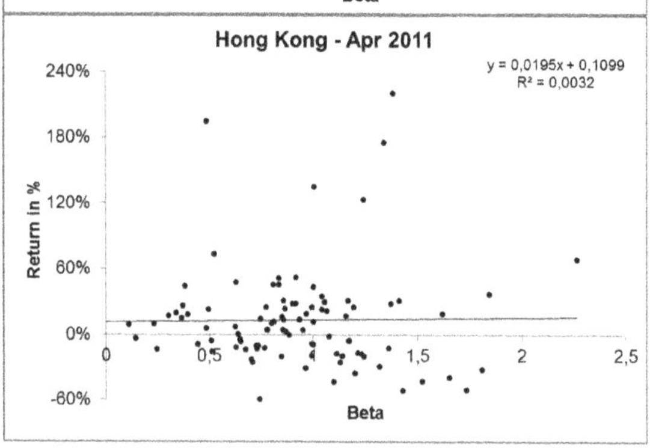
Hong Kong - Apr 2011
y = 0,0195x + 0,1099
R² = 0,0032
240%
180%
120%
60%
0%
-60%
Return in %
0
0,5
1
1,5
2
2,5
Beta

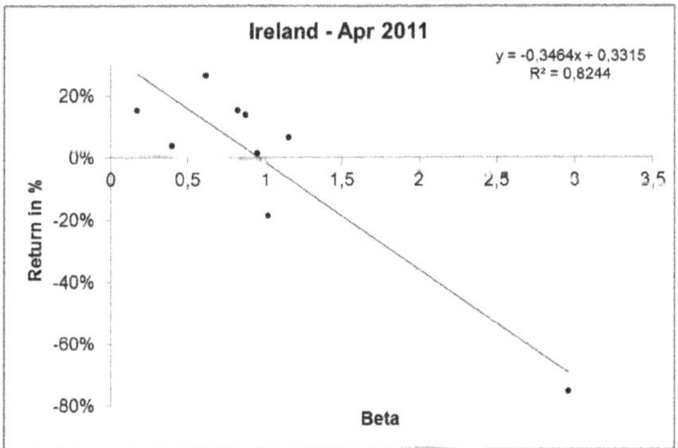
Ireland - Apr 2011
y = -0,3464x + 0,3315
R² = 0,8244
20%
0%
-20%
-40%
-60%
-80%
0
0,5
1
1,5
2
2,5
3
3,5
Return in %
Beta

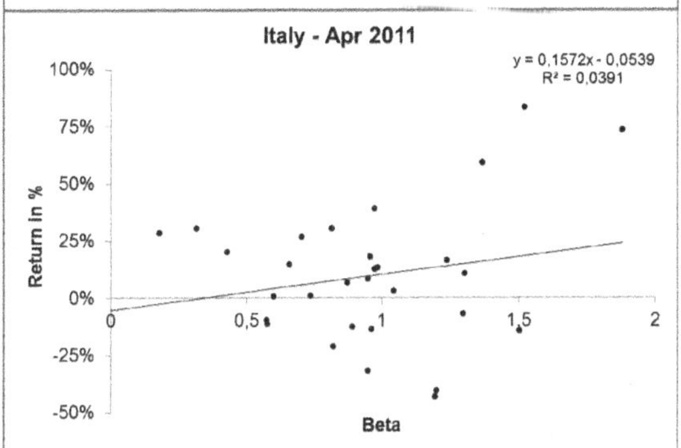
Italy - Apr 2011
y = 0,1572x - 0,0539
R² = 0,0391
100%
75%
50%
25%
0%
-25%
-50%
0
0,5
1
1,5
2
Return in %
Beta

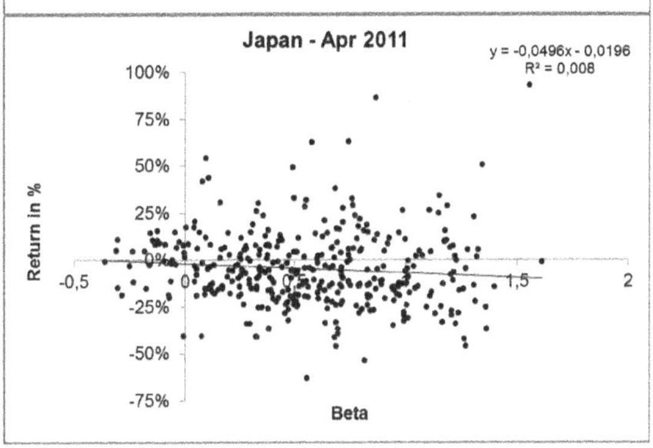
Japan - Apr 2011
y = -0,0496x - 0,0196
R² = 0,008
100%
75%
50%
25%
0%
-25%
-50%
-75%
-0,5
0
0,5
1
1,5
2
Return in %
Beta

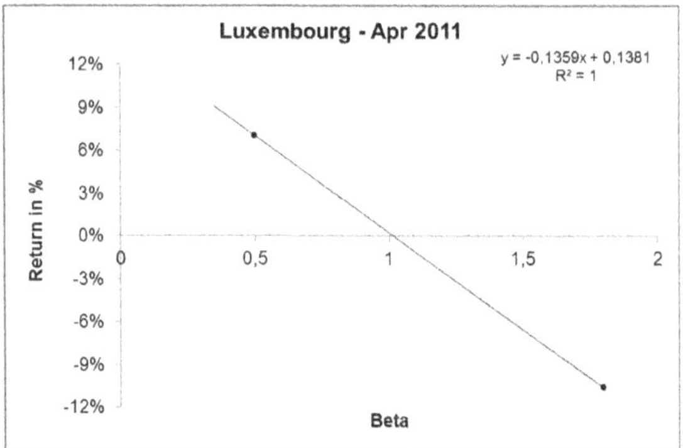
Luxembourg - Apr 2011
y = -0,1359x + 0,1381
R² = 1
12%
9%
6%
3%
0%
-3%
-6%
-9%
-12%
0
0,5
1
1,5
2
Return in %
Beta

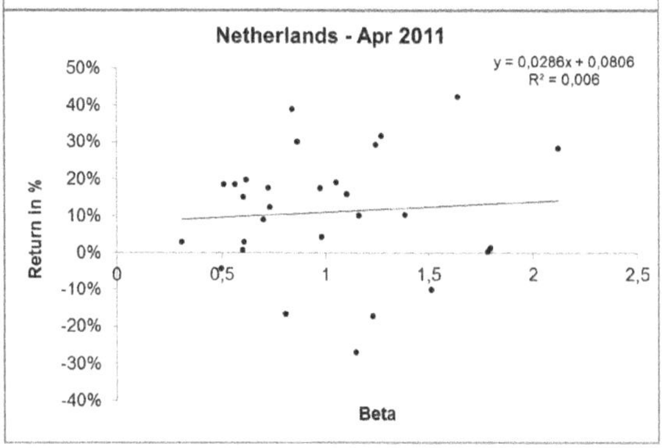
Netherlands - Apr 2011
y = 0,0286x + 0,0806
R² = 0,006
50%
40%
30%
20%
10%
0%
-10%
-20%
-30%
-40%
0
0,5
1
1,5
2
2,5
Return in %
Beta

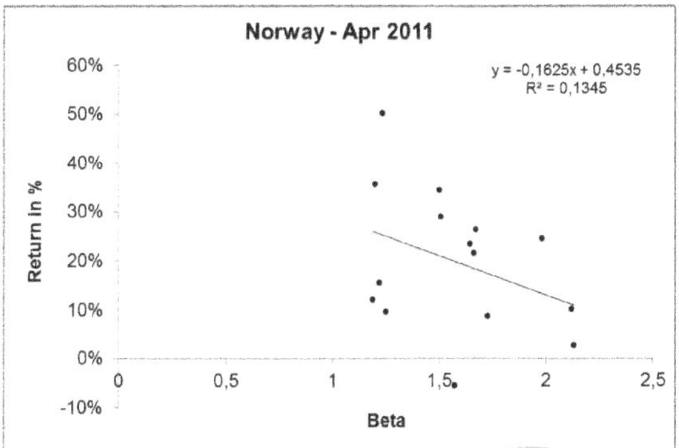
Norway - Apr 2011
y = -0,1625x + 0,4535
R² = 0,1345
60%
50%
40%
30%
20%
10%
0%
-10%
Return in %
0
0,5
1
1,5
2
2,5
Beta

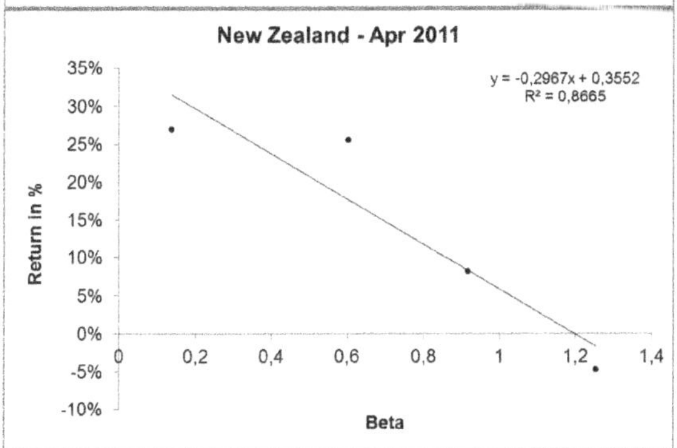
New Zealand - Apr 2011
y = -0,2967x + 0,3552
R² = 0,8665
35%
30%
25%
20%
15%
10%
5%
0%
-5%
-10%
Return in %
0
0,2
0,4
0,6
0,8
1
1,2
1,4
Beta

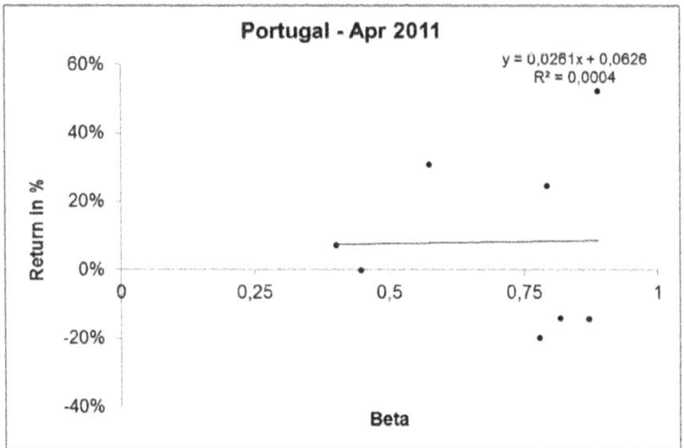
Portugal - Apr 2011
y = 0,0261x + 0,0626
R² = 0,0004
60%
40%
20%
0%
-20%
-40%
Return in %
0
0,25
0,5
0,75
1
Beta

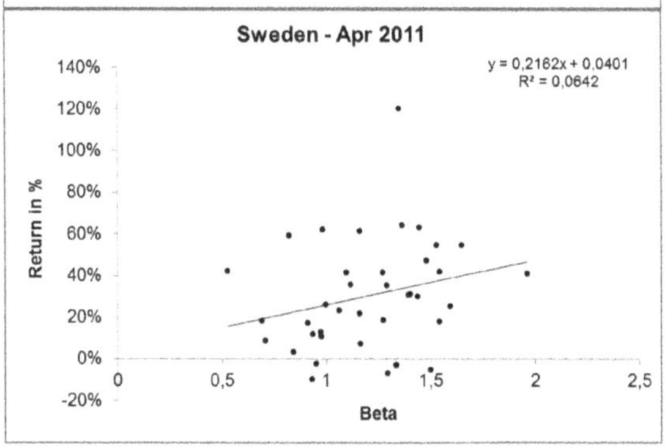
Sweden - Apr 2011
y = 0,2162x + 0,0401
R² = 0,0642
140%
120%
100%
80%
60%
40%
20%
0%
-20%
Return in %
0
0,5
1
1,5
2
2,5
Beta

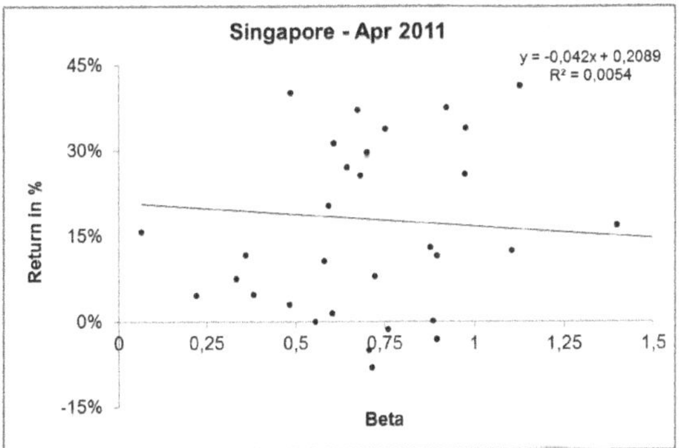
Singapore - Apr 2011
y = -0,042x + 0,2089
R² = 0,0054
45%
30%
15%
0%
-15%
Return in %
0
0,25
0,5
0,75
1
1,25
1,5
Beta

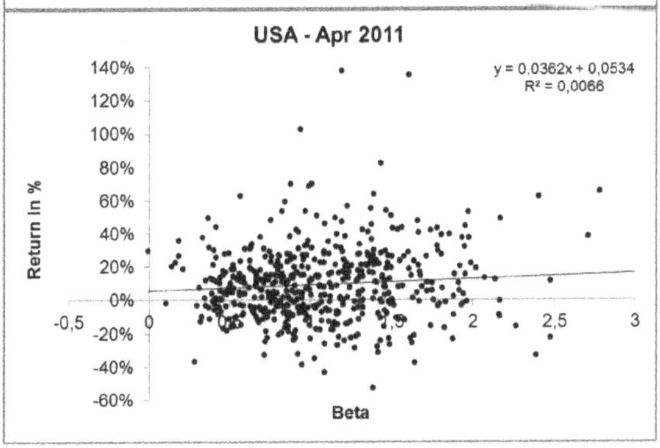
USA - Apr 2011
y = 0,0362x + 0,0534
R² = 0,0066
140%
120%
100%
80%
60%
40%
20%
0%
-20%
-40%
-60%
Return in %
-0,5
0
2
2,5
3
Beta

## Appendix 4: Risk-Return Relations of the Portfolio models

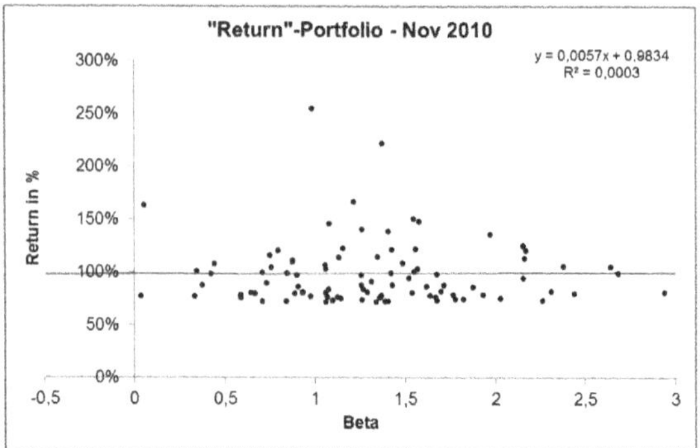


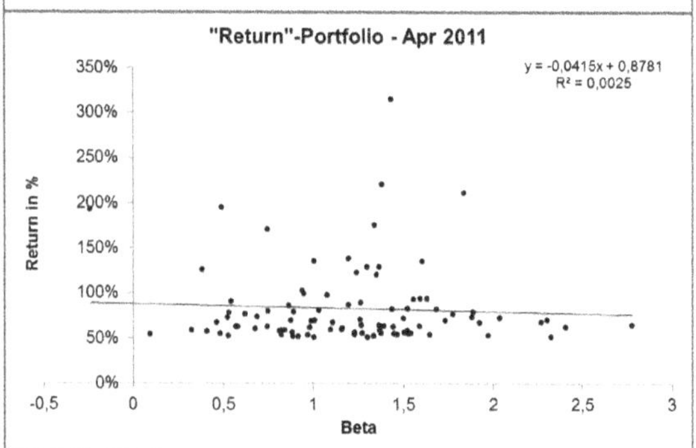


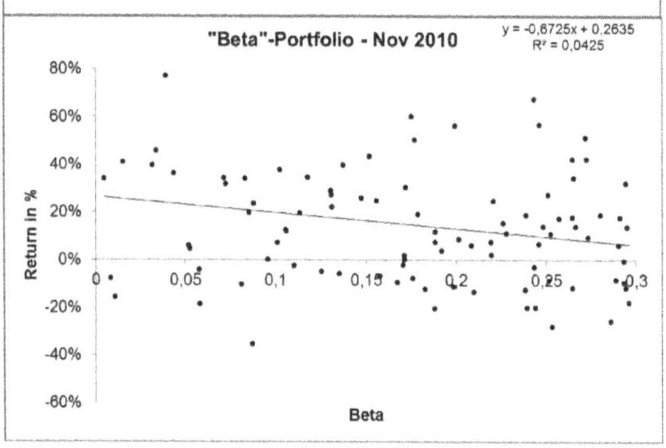

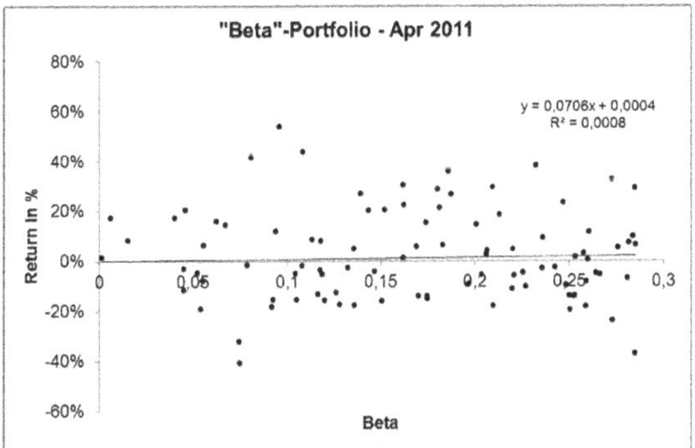
"Beta"-Portfolio - Apr 2011
y = 0,0706x + 0,0004
R² = 0,0008
80%
60%
40%
20%
0%
-20%
-40%
-60%
Return in %
0
0,05
0,1
0,15
0,2
0,25
0,3
Beta

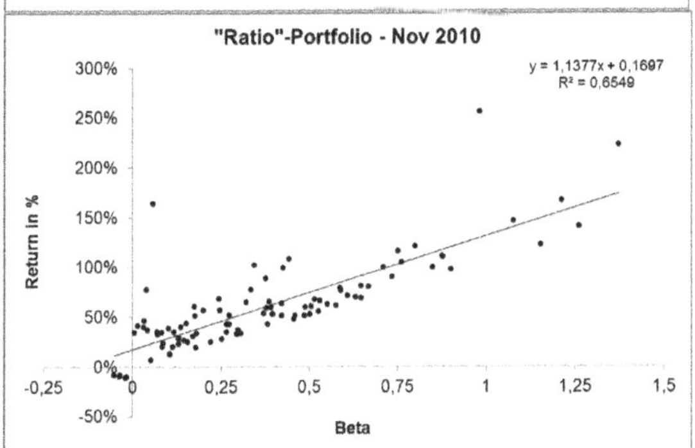
"Ratio"-Portfolio - Nov 2010
y = 1,1377x + 0,1697
R² = 0,6549
300%
250%
200%
150%
100%
50%
0%
-50%
Return in %
-0,25
0
0,25
0,5
0,75
1
1,25
1,5
Beta

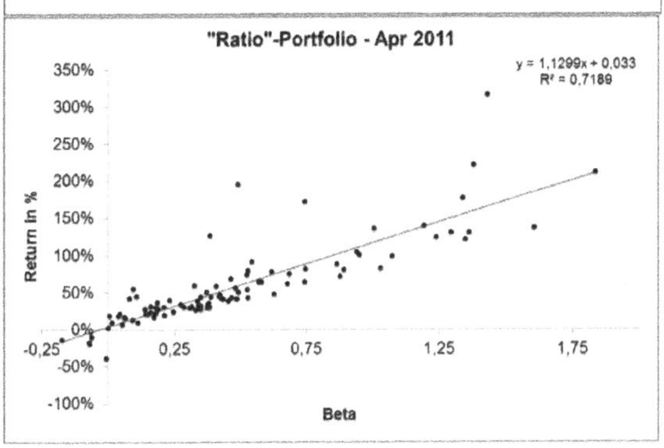
"Ratio"-Portfolio - Apr 2011
y = 1,1299x + 0,033
R² = 0,7189
350%
300%
250%
200%
150%
100%
50%
0%
-50%
-100%
Return in %
-0,25
0,25
0,75
1,25
1,75
Beta

# References


Allianz Global Investors, (2009). Branchen im Zyklus. Available from: http://www.allianzglobalinvestors.de/web/download?file=PortfolioPraxis-Konjunktur-II.pdf [accessed: 30th June 2011].

Ardalan, K., (2003). Theories and controversies in finance: a paradigmatic overview. *International Journal of Social Economics.* **30** (1/2), pp.199-209.

Bachelier, L.J.B.A., (1900). *Théorie de la speculation.* Paris: Gauthier-Villars. Reprinted in Cootner, P.H., (ed.) (1964). *The Random Character of Stock Market Prices.* Cambridge: MIT Press., pp.17-78.

Baltussen, G., (2008). *New Insights Into Behavioral Finance.* Ph.D.-Dissertation. Amsterdam: Rozenberg Publishers.

Banz, R.W., (1981). The Relationship Between Return and Market Value of Common Stocks. *Journal of Financial Economics.* **9** (1), pp.3-18.

Barberis, N., Shleifer, A., & Vishny, R., (1998). A model of investor sentiment. *Journal of Financial Economics.* **49** (3), pp.307-343.

Barberis,N., & Shleifer, A., (2003). Style investing. *Journal of Financial Economics.* **68** (2), pp.161-199.

Bettner, M.S., Robinson, C., & McGoun, E., (1994). The case for qualitative research in finance. *International Review of Financial Analysis.* **3** (1), pp.1-18.

Black, F. (1993). Beta and Return. *Journal of Portfolio Management.* **20** (1), pp.8-18.

Black, F., (1972). Capital Market Equilibrium with Restricted Borrowing. *Journal of Business.* **45** (3), pp.444-454.

Black, F., Jensen, M.C., & Scholes, M., (1972). The Capital Asset Pricing Model: Some Empirical Tests. **In:** Jensen, M.C. (ed.), Studies in the Theory of Capital Markets. New York: Praeger Publishers.

Brealey, R.A., & Myers, S.C., (2003). *Principles of Corporate Finance* (7th ed.). New York: McGraw-Hill.

Brealey, R.A., Myers, S.C., & Marcus, A.J., (2009). *Fundamentals of Corporate Finance* (6th ed.). New York: McGraw-Hill.

Breeden, D., (1979). An Intertemporal Asset Pricing Model with Stochastic Consumption and Investment Opportunities. *Journal of Financial Economics.* **7** (3), pp.265-296.

Brinson, G.P, Singer, B.D., & Beebower, G.L., (1991). Determinants of Portfolio Performance II: An Update. *Financial Analysts Journal.* **47** (3), p.40-48.

Bryman, A. & Bell, E., (2007). *Business Research Methods* (2nd ed.). Oxford: Oxford University Press.

Cajueiro, D.O., Gogas, P., & Tabak, B.M., (2009). Does financial market liberalization increase the degree of market efficiency? The case of the Athens stock exchange. *International Review of Financial Analysis.* **18** (1/2), pp.50-57.

Campbell, J.Y., Lo, A.W., & MacKinlay, A.C., (1997). *The Econometrics of Financial Markets*. Princeton: Princeton University Press.

Chan, K.C., (1986). *The Use of Information in Market Values for Estimating Time-Varying Stock Betas*. Working Paper, Faculty of Finance, Ohio State University.

Chan, K.C., (1987). *On the Return of the Contrarian Investment Strategy*. Working Paper, Faculty of Finance, Ohio State University.

Chordia, T., Roll, R. & Subrahmanyam, A. (2008). Liquidity and market efficiency. *Journal of Financial Economics*. **87** (2), pp.249-268.

Chordia, T., Roll. R., & Subrahmanyam, A., (2011). Recent Trends in trading activity and market quality. *Journal of Financial Economics*. **101** (2), pp.243-263.

Chung, D., & Hrazdil, K., (2010). Liquidity and market efficiency: A large sample study. *Journal of Banking & Finance*. **34** (10), pp.2346-2357.

Cohen, R.B., Polk, C., & Vuolteenaho, T., (2009). The Price Is (Almost) Right. *The Journal of Finance*. **64** (6), pp.2739-2782.

Connor, G., & Sehgal, S., (2001): *Tests of the Fama and French Model in India*. Working paper. London School of Economics.

Cootner, P.H., (1964). *The Random Character of Stock Market Prices*. Cambridge: MIT Press.

De Bondt, W.F.M., & Thaler, R.H., (1985). Does the Stock Market Overreact? *The Journal of Finance*. **40** (3), pp.793-805.

De Bondt, W.F.M., & Thaler, R.H., (1987). Further Evidence on Investor Overreaction and Stock Market Seasonality. *The Journal of Finance*. **42** (3), pp.557-581.

De Long, J.B, Shleifer, A., Summers, L.H., & Waldmann, R.J., (1990). Positive Feedback Investment Strategies and Destabilizing Rational Speculation.*The Journal of Finance*. **45** (2), pp.379-395.

Dhrymes, P.J., Friend, I., & Gultekin, N.B., (1984). A Critical Reexamination of the Empirical Evidence on the Arbitrage Pricing Theory. *The Journal of Finance*. **39** (2), pp.323-346.

Dicle, M.F., & Levendis, J., (2011). Greek market efficiency and its international integration. *Journal of International Financial Markets, Institutions & Money*. **21** (2), pp.229-246.

Dimson, E., & Mussavian, M., (1998). A brief history of market efficiency. *European Financial Management*. **4** (1), pp.91-103.

Dimson, E., & Mussavian, M., (1999). Three centuries of asset pricing. *Journal of Banking & Finance*. **23** (12), pp.1745-1769.

Elsas, R., El-Shaer, M.,& Theissen, E., (2003). Beta and returns revisited - Evidence from the German stock market. *Journal of International Financial Markets, Institutions & Money*. **13** (1), pp.1-18.

Elton, E., Gruber, M., & Mei, J., (1994). Cost of capital using arbitrage pricing theory: A case study of nine New York utilities. *Financial Markets, Institutions and Instruments*. **3** (3), pp.46–73.

Elton, E.J., & Gruber, M.J., (1977). Risk Reduction and Portfolio Size: An Analytical Solution. *Journal of Business*. **50** (4), pp.415-437.

Ernst & Young Global Ltd., (2011). *Global IPO trends 2011*. Available from: http://www.ey.com/Publication/vwLUAssets/Global-IPO-trends_2011/$FILE/Global%20IPO%20trends%202011.pdf [accessed: 30th June 2011].

Evans, J.L., & Archer, S.H., (1968). Diversification and the Reduction of Dispersion: An Empirical Analysis. *The Journal of Finance*. **23** (5), pp.761-767.

Fama E. F., & MacBeth, J.D., (1973). Risk, Return and Equilibrium: Empirical Tests. *The Journal of Political Economy*. **81** (3), pp.607-636.

Fama, E.F., & French, K.R., (1992). The cross-section of expected stock returns. *The Journal of Finance*. **47** (2), pp.427-465.

Fama, E.F., & French, K.R., (1997). Industry Costs of Equity. *Journal of Financial Economics*. **43** (2), pp.153-193.

Fama, E.F., & French, K.R., (2004). The Capital Asset Pricing Model: Theory and Evidence. *Journal of Economic Perspectives*. **18** (3), pp.25-46.

Fama, E.F., (11th August 2009). *Fama on Market Efficiency in a Volatile Market*. Available from: http://www.dimensional.com/famafrench/2009/08/fama-on-market-efficiency-in-a-volatile-market.html [accessed 30th May 2011].

Fama, E.F., (1965). The Behavior of Stock-Market Prices. *The Journal of Business*. **38** (1), pp.34-105.

Fama, E.F., (1970). Efficient Capital Markets: A Review of Theory and Empirical Work. *The Journal of Finance*. **25** (2), pp.383-417.

Fama, E.F., (1998). Market efficiency, long-term returns, and behavioral finance. *Journal of Financial Economics*. **49** (3), pp.283-306.

Fama, E.F., Fisher, L., Jensen, M., & Roll, R. (1969). The Adjustment of Stock Prices to New Information. *International Economic Review*. **10** (1), pp.1-21.

Fletcher, J., (2000). On the conditional relationship between beta and return in international stock markets. *International Review of Financial Analysis*. **9** (3), pp.235-245.

Fluck, Z., Malkiel, B., & Quandt, R., (1997). The Predictability of Stock Returns: A Cross-Sectional Simulation. *The Review of Economics and Statistics*. **79** (2), pp.176-183.

Fraser, P., Hamelink, F., Hoesli, M., & MacGregor, B., (2004). Time-varying betas and cross-sectional return-risk relation: evidence from the UK. *European Journal of Finance*. **10** (4), pp.255-276.

Freeman, M.C., & Guermat, C., (2006). The conditional relationship between beta and returns: a re-assessment. *Journal of Business Finance and Accounting*. **33** (7/8), pp.1213-1239.

Friedman, M. (1975). *There's No Such Thing as a Free Lunch – Essays on Public Policy*. LaSalle: Open Court Publishing.

Graham, B., (1959). *The Intelligent Investor – A Practical Counsel* (3rd ed.). New York: Harper & Brothers Publishers.

Grinblatt, M., & Titman, S., (1989). Mutual fund performance: An analysis of quarterly portfolio holdings. *Journal of Business*. **62** (3), pp.394-415.

Hansen, L.P., & Richard, S.F., (1987). The Role of Conditioning Information in Deducing Testable Restrictions Implied by Dynamic Asset Pricing Model. *Econometrica*. **55** (3), pp.587-613.

Ho, R.Y., Strange, R., & Piesse, J. (2006): On the conditional pricing effects of beta, size, and book-to-market equity in the Hong Kong market. *Journal of International Financial Markets, Institutions and Money*. **16** (3), pp.199-214

Huberman, G., & Wang, Z., (2005). *Arbitrage Pricing Theory*. Federal Reserve Bank of New York Staff Reports, no. 216.

Ibbotson Associates, (1985). *Stocks, Bonds, Bills, and Inflation: 1985 Yearbook*. Chicago: Ibbotson Associates, Inc.

Ibbotson, R.G., & Kaplan, P.D., (2000). Does Asset Allocation Policy Explain 40, 90, 100 Percent of Performance? *Financial Analysts Journal*. **56** (1), pp.26-33.

Isakov, D., (1999). Is beta still alive? Conclusive evidence from the Swiss stock market. *European Journal of Finance*. **5** (3), pp.202-212.

Jegadeesh, N., & Titman, S., (1993). Returns to Buying Winners and Selling Losers: Implications for Stock Market Efficiency. *The Journal of Finance*. **48** (1), pp.65-91.

Jegadeesh, N., & Titman, S., (2001). Profitability of Momentum Strategies: An Evaluation of Alternative Explanations. *The Journal of Finance*. **56** (2), pp.699-720.

Jensen, M.C., (1978). Some Anomalous Evidence Regarding Market Efficiency. *Journal of Financial Economics*. **6** (2/3), pp.95-101.

Jones, C.M., & Lamont, O.A., (2002). Short-sale constraints and stock returns. *Journal of Financial Economics*. **66** (2/3), pp.207-239.

Kahneman, D., & Tversky, A., (1979). Prospect Theory: An Analysis of Decision under Risk. *Econometrica*. **7** (2), pp.263-292.

Kahneman, D., Slovic, P., & Tversky, A., (1982). *Judgment Under Uncertainty: Heuristics and Biases*. London: Cambridge University Press.

Keim, D.B., (1983). Size Related Anomalies and Stock Return Seasonality. *Journal of Financial Economics*. **12** (1), pp. 13-32.

Kendall, M.G., (1953). The analysis of economic time-series-part I: Prices. *Journal of the Royal Statistical Society. Series A (General)*. **116** (1), pp.11-34.

Kent, D., & Titman, S., (1997). Evidence on the Characteristics of Cross-Sectional Variation in Stock Returns. *The Journal of Finance*. **52** (1), pp.1-33.

Krugman, P.R., & Obstfeld, M., (2008). *International Economics: Theory and Policy* ($8^{th}$ ed.). Amsterdam: Addison-Wesley Longman.

Lakonishok, J., Shleifer, A., & Vishny, R.W., (1994). Contrarian Investment, Extrapolation, and Risk. *The Journal of Finance*. **49** (5), pp.1541-1578.

Lamont, O.A., & Thaler, R.H., (2003). Can the Market Add and Substract? Mispricing in Tech Stock Carve Outs. *The Journal of Political Economy*. **111** (2), pp.227-268.

LeRoy, S.F., (1989). Efficient Capital Markets and Martingales. *Journal of Economic Literature*. **27** (4), pp.1583-1621.

Lévy, P., (1925). *Calcul des Probabilités.* Paris: Gauthier-Villars.

Levy, R.A., (1967). Relative Strength as a Criterion for Investment Selection. *The Journal of Finance*. **22** (4), pp.595-610.

Lintner, J., (1965a). The Valuation of Risk Assets and the Selection of Risky Investments in Stock Portfolios and Capital Budgets. *The Review of Economics and Statistics.* **47** (1), pp.13-37.

Lintner, J., (1965b). Securities Prices, Risk, and Maximal Gains from Diversification. *The Journal of Finance*. **20** (4), pp.587-615.

Lo, A.W., & MacKinlay, A.C., (1988) Stock Market Prices Do Not Follow Random Walks: Evidence from a Simple Specification Test. *The Review of Financial Studies*. **1** (1), pp.41-66.

Lucas, R.E.jr., (1978). Asset Prices in an Exchange Economy. *Econometrica*. **46** (6), pp.1429-1445.

Malkiel, B.G., (2003). The Efficient Market Hypothesis and Its Critics. *Journal of Economic Perspectives*. **17** (1), pp.59-82.

Mandelbrot, B., (1963). The Variation of Certain Speculative Prices. *The Journal of Business*. **36** (4), pp.394-419.

Mankiw, N.G., (2011). *Principles of Economics* (6th ed.). Mason: South-Western Cengage Learning.

Markowitz, H.M., (1952). Portfolio Selection. *The Journal of Finance*. **7** (1), pp.77-91.

Markowitz, H.M., (1956). The Optimization of a Quadratic Function Subject to Linear Constraints. *Naval Research Logistics Quarterly*, **3** (1/2), pp.111-133.

Markowitz, H.M., (1959). *Portfolio Selection, Efficient Diversification of Investments*. New York: John Wiley and Sons.

Markowitz, H.M., (1999). The Early History of Portfolio Theory: 1600-1960. *Financial Analysts Journal*. **55** (4), pp.5-16.

Mergner, S., & Bulla, J., (2008), Time-varying beta risk of pan-European industry portfolios: A comparison of alternative modeling techniques. *European Journal of Finance*. **14** (8), pp.771-802.

Merton, R.C., (1969). Lifetime Portfolio Selection under Uncertainty: The Continuous-Time Case. The Review of Economics and Statistics. **51** (3), pp.247-257.

Merton, R.C., (1971). Optimum Consumption and Portfolio Rules in a Continuous-time Model. *Journal of Economic Theory*. **3** (4), pp.373-413.

Merton, R.C., (1973). An Intertemporal Capital Asset Pricing Model. *Econometrica*. **41** (5), pp. 867-887.

Miller, E.M., (1977). Risk, Uncertainty, and Divergence of Opinion. *The Journal of Finance*. **32** (4), pp.1151-1168.

Modigliani, F., & Pogue G.A., (1973). *An introduction to risk and return concepts and evidence*. Working paper no.646-673. Cambridge: Sloan School of Management.

Moore, A., (1962). *A Statistical Analysis of Common-Stock Prices*, unpublished Ph.D. dissertation, Graduate School of Business, University of Chicago.

Mossin, J., (1966). Equilibrium in a Capital Asset Market. *Econometrica*. **34** (4), pp.768-783.

Niederhoffer, V., & Osborne, M.F.M., (1966). Market Making and Reversal on the Stock Exchange. *Journal of the American Statistical Association*. **61** (316), pp.897-916.

Odean, T., (1998). Are Investors Reluctant to Realize their Losses? *The Journal of Finance*. **53** (5), pp.1775-1798.

Odier, P., & Solnik, B., (1993). Lessons for International Asset Allocation. *Financial Analysts Journal*. **49** (2), pp.69-77.

Osborne, M.F.M., (1959). Brownian Motion in the Stock Market. *Operations Research*. **7** (2), pp.145-173.

Pettengill, G. N., Sundaram, S., & Mathur, I., (1995). The conditional relation between beta and returns. *Journal of Financial and Quantitative Analysis*. **30** (1), pp.101-116.

Pietzsch, L., (2004). Bestimmungsfaktoren der Analysten-Coverage – Eine empirische Analyse für den deutschen Kapitalmarkt. Ph.D.-dissertation. Bad Soden: Uhlenbruch Verlag.

Popović, T., (2004). *Customer Capital – Die Wertschöpfung von E-Commerce-Unternehmen und ihre zweckadäquate Bewertung aus Perspektive des Aktienresearch*. Ph.D.-dissertation. Sternenfels: Verlag Wissenschaft & Praxis.

Popper, K.R., (1934). *Logik der Forschung*. Tübingen: Mohr Siebeck.

Reinganum, M.R., (1983). The Anomalous Stock Market Behavior of Small Firms in January: Empirical Tests for Tax-Loss Selling Effects. *Journal of Financial Economics*. **12** (1), pp.89-104.

Roberts, Harry (1967). *Statistical Versus Clinical Prediction of the Stock Market*. Unpublished manuscript, Center for Research in Security Prices, Booth School of Business, University of Chicago, Chicago.

Roll, R.W, & Ross, S.A., (1980). An Empirical Investigation of the Arbitrage Pricing Theory. *The Journal of Finance*. **35** (5), pp.1073-1103.

Roll, R.W., (1977). A Critique of the Asset Pricing Theory's Tests: Part I: On Past and Potential Testability of the Theory. *Journal of Financial Economics*. **4** (2), pp.129-176.

Ross, S.A., (1976). The Arbitrage Theory of Capital Asset Pricing. *Journal of Economic Theory*. **13** (3), pp.341-360.

Roy, A.D., (1952). Safety First and the Holding of Assets. *Econometrica*. **20** (3), pp.431-449.

Rozeff, M.S.,& Zaman, M.A., (1988). Market Efficiency and Insider Trading: New Evidence. *The Journal of Business*. **61** (1), pp.25-44.

Rubinstein, M., (1973). The Fundamental Theorem of Parameter-Preference Security Valuation. *Journal of Financial and Quantitative Analysis.* **8** (1), pp.61-69.

Rubinstein, M., (1976). The Valuation of Uncertain Income Streams and the Pricing of Options. *The Boll Journal of Economics.* **7** (2), pp.407-425.

Samuelson, P A. (1965). Proof that properly anticipated prices fluctuate randomly *Industrial Management Review.* **6** (2), pp.41-49.

Samuelson, P.A., (1967). General Proof that Diversification Pays. *Journal of Financial and Quantitative Analysis.* **2** (1), pp.1-13.

Saunders, M., Lewis, P., & Thornhill, A., (2007). Research Methods for Business Students (4th ed.). London: Prentice Hall.

Schwert, G.W., (2003). Anomalies and market efficiency. **In:** Constantinidis, G.M., Harris, M., & Stulz, R.M., (Eds): *Handbook of the Economics of Finance.* Amsterdam: North-Holland, pp. 937-972.

Sewell, M., (2011), *History of the efficient market hypothesis.* Research Note RN/11/04, University College London, London.

Sharpe, W., (1966). Mutual fund performance. *Journal of Business.* **39** (1), pp.119–138.

Sharpe, W.F., (1963). A Simplified Model for Portfolio Analysis. *Management Science.* **9** (2), pp.277-293.

Sharpe, W.F., (1964). Capital asset prices: a theory of market equilibrium under conditions of risk. *The Journal of Finance.* **19** (3), pp.425-442.

Shiller, R.J., (2003). From Efficient Markets Theory to Behavioral Finance. *Journal of Economic Perspectives.* **17** (1), pp.83-104.

Solnik, B.H., (1974). Why Not Diversify Internationally Rather Than Domestically. *Financial Analysts Journal.* **30** (4), pp.48-54.

Spremann, K., (2008). *Portfoliomanagement* (4th ed.). München: Oldenbourg.

Statman, M., & Shefrin, H., (1985). The Disposition to Sell Winners too Early and Ride Losers too long: Theory and Evidence. *The Journal of Finance.* **40** (3), pp.777-790.

Statman, M., (1987). How Many Stocks Make a Diversified Portfolio? *Journal of Financial and Quantitative Analysis.* **22** (3), pp.353-363.

STOXX Limited, (2011). *STOXX Global 1800 Automobiles & Parts.* Available from: http://www.stoxx.com/indices/index_information.html?symbol=SXW1ATOE [accessed: 28th March 2011].

Tang, G.Y., & Shum, W.C., (2003). The conditional relationship between beta and returns: recent evidence from international stock market. *International Business Review.* **12** (1), pp.109-126.

Tobin, J., (1958). Liquidity Preference as Behavior Towards Risk. *The Review of Economic Studies.* **25** (2), pp.65-86.

Tobin, J., (1958). Liquidity Preference as Behaviour Towards Risk. *The Review of Economic Studies.* **25** (2), pp.65-86.

Treynor, J.L., (1961). *Toward a Theory of Market Value of Risky Assets.* Unpublished manuscript, **in:** Dimson, E., & Mussavian, M., (eds) (1998). *Foundations of Finance Volume II: Asset Pricing.* Aldershot: Dartmouth Publishing Company.

Treynor, Jack (1965). How to Rate Management of Investment Funds. *Harvard Business Review,* **43** (1), pp. 63-75.

Tversky, A., & Kahneman, D., (1974). Judgement under Uncertainty: Heuristics and Biases. *Science.* **185** (4157), pp.1124-1131.

Vermaelen, T. & Verstringe, M., (1986). *Do Belgians Overreact?* Working Paper, Catholic University of Louvain, Belgium.

Weber, M., (1947). *The Theory of Social and Economic Organization.* Translated by Henderson, A.M., & Parsons, T. New York: Free Press.

Youssef, H.B.M.H, El Moubarki, L., & Sioud, O.B., (2010). Can diversification degree amplify momentum and contrarian anomalies? Review of Accounting and Finance. **9** (1), pp.50-64.

CPSIA information can be obtained
at www.ICGtesting.com
Printed in the USA
LVOW05s1941220817
545961LV00015B/279/P

9 783658 066338